FROM EGYPT TO MESOPOTAMIA

FROM EGYPT TO MESOPOTAMIA

A STUDY OF PREDYNASTIC TRADE ROUTES

• SAMUEL MARK •

Texas A&M University Press
College Station

CHATHAM PUBLISHING

LONDON

Published in Great Britain in 1998 by
Chatham Publishing
1 & 2 Faulkner's Alley
Cowcross Street
London ECIM 6DD
Chatham Publishing is an imprint of
Gerald Duckworth & Co Ltd

The paper used in this book meets the minimum requirements
of the American National Standard for Permanence
of Paper for Printed Library Materials, Z39.48-1984.
Binding materials have been chosen for durability.

Library of Congress Cataloging-in-Publication Data

Mark, Samuel.
From Egypt to Mesopotamia : a study of predynastic trade routes /
Samuel Mark. — 1st ed.
p.   cm. — (Studies in nautical archaeology ; no. 4)
Includes bibliographical references and index.
ISBN 0-89096-777-6 (alk. paper)
1. Egypt—Antiquities. 2. Middle East—Antiquities. 3. Underwater
archaeology—Middle East. 4. Egypt—Commerce—Iraq. 5. Iraq—
Commerce—Egypt. I. Title. II. Series.
DT60.M36   1997
382´.0939´4—dc21   97-21879
                                                          CIP

British Library Cataloguing in Publication Data
A catalogue record for this book is available from the British Library
Chatham ISBN 1-86176-066-3

*To my parents
and all my siblings
without whose
love and support
this work could not
have been completed.*

CONTENTS

FIGURES

TABLES

ACKNOWLEDGMENTS

This work represents a long and sometimes arduous journey that I would not have been able to complete without the help of others. I must thank Linda Blair and the staff of the Learning Resources Department, who made it possible for me to print out countless rough drafts of this manuscript; to Margaret Carpenter and the staff of the Interlibrary Services Department for acquiring many hard-to-find books and journals; to Del Lockhart and the staff of Graphic Arts for helping me prepare fifty-six ink and mylar drawings for publication; and to the staff of the Texas A&M University Press. I am indebted to Anne Lesseman, Frederick H. van Doorninck, and Shelley Wachsmann for their advice and guidance, and to McGuire Gibson and Mark Lehner of the University of Chicago for making many valuable suggestions. I am particularly grateful to George F. Bass and Michael A. Fitzgerald, without their help this work would never have been published. Although I am deeply indebted for the help given by my friends and colleagues, I alone am responsible for all of the opinions and errors that appear in this manuscript. This disclaimer is extended to the line drawings. Because all fifty-six line drawings were produced by my hand, I must accept responsibility for any errors.

FROM EGYPT TO MESOPOTAMIA

INTRODUCTION

The possible influence of Mesopotamia on the development of pre-dynastic Egypt has intrigued scholars for most of this century.[1] Henri Frankfort, who made the first comprehensive study of Egyptian and Mesopotamian relations, believed that Asiatic peoples came to Egypt from Mesopotamia via the Red Sea near the Wadi Hammamat, where they were accepted by the native population. In so doing, he believed, they introduced a number of objects and motifs into ancient Egyptian culture.[2] Following Frankfort, Helene Kantor became the main proponent of this theory, not only refining it but also calling attention to other artifacts of Mesopotamian derivation.[3] Subsequent supporters of a predynastic connection between Egypt and Mesopotamia include Elise Baumgartel and William Ward.[4] In spite of opposition,[5] the evidence for at least indirect trade between Mesopotamia and Egypt appears irrefutable. These proponents of Mesopotamian influence on predynastic and early dynastic Egypt have devoted numerous pages to it but have seldom expended more than a paragraph or so to the possible trade routes that allowed goods and influences to flow between these two cultures. What we are told of such routes is, more often than not, based on opinion instead of archaeological evidence.

Two possible routes have been proposed, a northern route through Syria-Palestine that continued, either by land or by sea, to Egypt;[6] and a southern route by sea through the Persian Gulf, around Saudi Arabia, up the Red Sea to the Wadi Hammamat, and, finally, by land to Naqada (fig. 1).[7] A direct route linking southern Mesopotamia with Palestine seems untenable because the camel, which even-

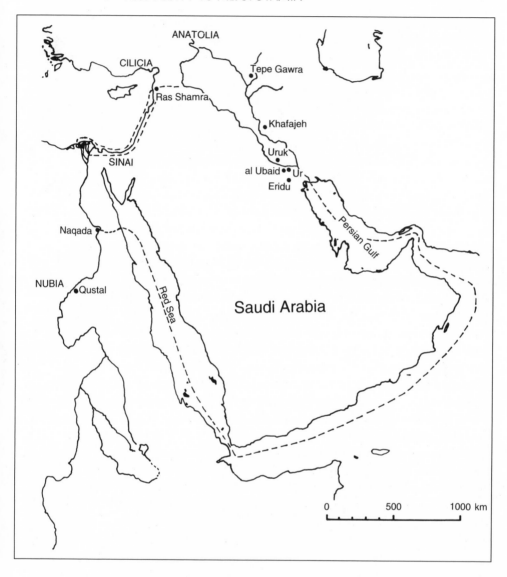

Fig. 1. Possible Trade Routes, ca. 3500–3100 B.C.

tually made this route viable, was not used as a pack animal at this early date.[8]

Evidence for a southern route consists primarily of the "foreign ship" pictographs studied by Hans Winkler in and near the Wadi Hammamat,[9] and the distribution of Mesopotamian artifacts and motifs in southern Egypt.[10] The possibility of a northern route is supported by the fact that predynastic trade between Egypt and Syria-

Palestine roughly coincides with the expansion of Mesopotamian influence into Syria during the Protoliterate period.[11]

This study attempts to reconstruct the avenues of trade between predynastic Egypt and protoliterate Mesopotamia by plotting the respective distributions of their artifacts, motifs, and raw materials. Prior to an evaluation of these features, a general review of Egyptian and Mesopotamian archaeology and trade may help clarify the nature of the relations and connections between such distant areas. Extant studies present the evidence for trade between these two areas as if it was trade between two homogeneous cultures, but this review will underscore the fact that in each region two distinct cultures evolved. Consequently, as we evaluate the evidence for trade between Egypt and Mesopotamia, it will be important to recognize that we are attempting to reconstruct trade patterns between two different groups in both Egypt and Mesopotamia and possibly between a number of other peoples who separated them.

2 HISTORY AND TRADE
OF EARLY MESOPOTAMIA

The Ubaid culture (ca. 5300–4000 B.C.) (table 1) extended through-out northern and southern Mesopotamia (fig. 2). In the early phases of the Ubaid period, the people still relied on hunting and fishing for subsistence, but, as time passed, farming replaced hunting as the basis of the economy. Rectangular mud-brick houses eventually took the place of circular mud-covered huts, and temples evolved from simple rectangular structures to tripartite temples with niched fa-cades. Metal was rare; flint, chert, and obsidian were used to make tools, weapons, and some vessels. In the south, because of a scarcity of stone, sickles and axes were made of hard-baked clay. Most mate-rial aspects of culture improved during the Ubaid period, though the quality of most pottery declined.[1]

In the north, Ubaid influence spread well beyond Mesopotamian borders. Ubaid or Ubaid-style pottery is found at various sites across northern Syria as far west as Ras Shamra, and in southern Anatolia.[2] Because this pottery is found along routes leading to mining areas in Anatolia, it may signify importation of raw materials into Mesopota-mia.[3] Degirmentepe, for example, a site in southern Anatolia on a route to both copper and silver deposits, is believed to have been an Ubaid "outpost" because its painted pottery, dwelling type, and thousands of clay seals or *bullae* reflect Ubaid influence (fig. 2).[4]

To the south, Ubaid pottery, most of it from Ur, al Ubaid, and Eridu in southern Mesopotamia, has been found on as many as fifty sites around the Persian Gulf. It has been proposed that the absence of any evidence for permanent structures or trade at these sites sug-gests that this pottery marks places used only seasonally by early Mesopotamian fishermen.[5] Michael Roaf and Jane Galbraith have re-

Table 1: Relative Chronologies

Lower Egypt	Upper Egypt	Palestine	Tell Judeidah	Middle Euphrates	Tell Brak	Tepe Gawra	Southern Mesopotamia	Byblos
First Dynasty		EB II	Phase G		Grey Eye Temple	VIII C	Jamdat Nasr	
Buto	N III	EB I		Habuba Kabira			Late Uruk	énéolithique ancien
Maadi / Complex	N II c/d	Ghassulian	Phase F			IX		
	N II a/b					X	Middle Uruk	
	N I					XI-A		
Omari A						XII	Early Uruk	
Merimde / Fayum A	Badarian					XIII	Ubaid	
			Phase E					

examined the data and agree that most of the Ubaid pottery found in the gulf may have been imported from southern Mesopotamia. But they also point out that few sites have Ubaid pottery, that these sites were mostly small and occupied for short periods and at widely different times, that Ubaid pots were frequently mended, and that other characteristic Ubaid artifacts are rare on gulf sites. Therefore, no evidence exists to suggest large-scale trade or the establishment of seasonal villages to harvest fish, shells, or pearls by Ubaid traders or fishermen. Instead, Roaf and Galbraith propose that the argument for long-distance trade has been overstated and that a more modest trade in fish, grain, and textiles between Mesopotamian and gulf sites over a longer period is best supported by the evidence.[6] It should also be noted that as late as about 4900 B.C., the sea level in the gulf was approximately four meters lower than it is at present,[7] and Arabia was in a major subpluvial phase.[8] Such conditions may have permitted a more southerly distribution of Ubaid settlements,[9] and may have been more favorable for trade via a land route.

Sorghum, which was found at a site in Oman, is cited as evidence

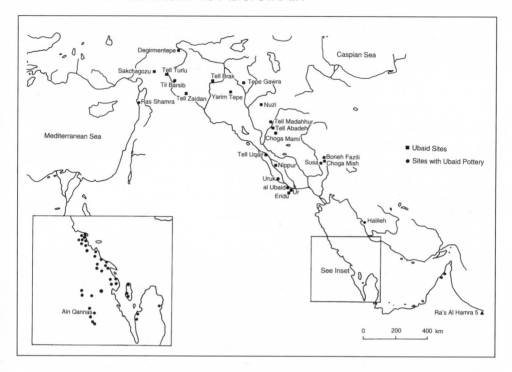

Fig. 2. Distribution of Ubaid Sites

suggesting trade with Africa.[10] Sorghum is a cereal grass that is thought to have been originally domesticated in the Ethiopian-Sudanese region. Because the sorghum in Oman was found at what is believed to have been a seasonal fishing camp known as Ra's al Hamra 5 (fig. 2), it is proposed that it was transported there via watercraft from Ethiopia or Egypt. We must remember, however, that Arabia was in a major subpluvial phase at this time and that such a climate may have been conducive to the growing of sorghum at a nearby location.[11] Furthermore, even if we could prove that domesticated sorghum came to southern Arabia by sea, sorghum would not be evidence of contact with Egypt, because the plant is not known in Egypt before approximately 2000 B.C.[12] and does not appear to have been widely cultivated there until about A.D. 100.[13] We must, therefore, be cautious about citing sorghum as evidence of contact until more information is available.

The Ubaid culture was succeeded by the Gawra culture in the north (ca. 4000–3100 B.C.) and the Uruk culture in the south (ca. 4000–3100 B.C.). Tepe Gawra in northern Mesopotamia imported lapis lazuli, ivory, turquoise, jadeite, carnelian, hematite, obsidian, quartz, and diorite, presumably from Anatolia, Iran, and Armenia. Gold items are abundant, and cast copper objects such as buttons, chisels, awls, and pins become more common. As in Iran, during the Gawra period, red, green, and blue pigments are found in burials, and as in the south, the tripartite temple with niched facade was characteristic.[14]

The Uruk period was a time of increased growth, complexity, and centralization of society. The importance of religion is reflected in the ever-increasing size and wealth of its temples, which are based on the tripartite-and-niched-facade design of the Ubaid period. During the later phases of the Uruk period, the niches were filled with mosaics made of clay cones; each cone was painted red, white, or black. Cone-mosaics also decorated columns and walls. The labor-intensive use of thousands of such cones for each temple, combined with the expanded utilization of various stones and metals, indicate increased labor specialization, as is illustrated also by beautifully carved stone vases, stelae, and cylinder seals. Luxury goods made of various metals became more common, and, by the end of the period, the lost-wax technique of casting was widely employed. Finally, the degree of labor specialization in and social centralization of southern Mesopotamia is best exemplified by the development of writing, which was in response to the need to keep records of increasing volume of goods being produced and traded.[15]

Because southern Mesopotamia was poor in natural resources, most stone-, metal-, and wood-working materials had to be imported. It is believed that, in return, cloth, wool garments, cereals, dried fish, leather, and finished goods were exported.[16] The need for raw materials may have provided the stimulus for the establishment of Mesopotamian "colonies" at Habuba Kabira/Tell Qannas and Jebel Aruda in northern Syria during the Late Uruk, or Uruk IV, period.[17] At this same time, Arslantepe, Tepecik, and Hassek Höyük show strong Mesopotamian influences.[18] This is also true of Norşuntepe, which is located in an area rich in copper and silver in southern Anatolia and has produced evidence of a well-developed metal industry.[19] By the end of the Uruk period, the inhabitants of these sites had either disappeared or had been assimilated by the indigenous population (fig. 3).

A thriving trade between both northern and southern Mesopotamia and Iranian sites appears to have been well established by the end of the Uruk period. Southern Mesopotamian trade around the Persian Gulf, on the other hand, seems to have been in its earliest

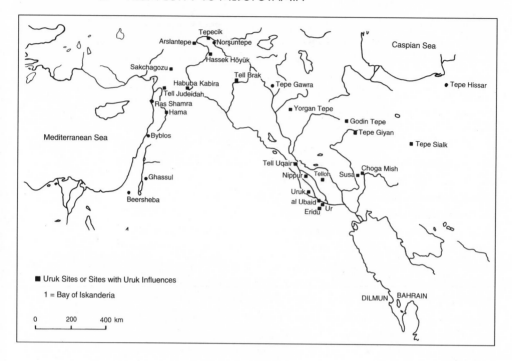

Fig. 3. Distribution of Late Uruk Sites

stages of development, for only a few artifacts from the late Uruk period have been found in this region, and these do not seem to appear south of the island of Bahrain.[20] The fact that such artifacts are so rare may be owing to a decrease in the sea level at the beginning of the Uruk period followed by a rise in sea level at the end of the period, which would have covered the coastal sites. The scarcity of finds, however, may have another explanation. Dilmun is mentioned at least once in a Late Uruk recension of the Archaic lú list from Uruk. This list names a "Dilmun tax-collector."[21] If Dilmun encompassed Bahrain and the surrounding region, a region where most of the archaeological evidence has been found, then perhaps the trade that existed was simply centered in this area (fig. 3).

In the succeeding Jamdat Nasr period (ca. 3100–2900 B.C.), Mesopotamian contacts and influence seem to have shifted away from northern Syria, focusing more strongly on the Iranian and Persian Gulf areas, as suggested by an increase in textual references to Dilmun and a corresponding increase in the archaeological evidence in Saudi Arabia dating to this period. Jamdat Nasr-type pottery is found as far south as Oman, and, because Oman is rich in copper, it is possible that the Mesopotamians were attempting to exploit a new source of this metal, even though no sign appears in the texts that could be interpreted to mean Oman.[22] Therefore, the evidence suggests, even at this late date, that Mesopotamian trade was confined to an area that extended only as far south as Dilmun, and that Dilmun was the transshipment point between southern Mesopotamia and Oman.

3

HISTORY AND TRADE
OF PREDYNASTIC EGYPT

People of the Badarian culture (ca. 5000–4000 B.C.)[1] lived on the east side of the Nile Valley, extending north to Matmar and south to Hemamieh, but Badarian pottery may have been found as far south as Hierakonpolis (fig. 4). This culture is primarily known for the quality of its pottery, which is eggshell thin and very hard, indicating a high firing temperature, and has a rippled and highly burnished surface. Ivory, however, was a popular material from which were carved bracelets, beads, figurines, pots, pins, and combs. Most stone tools were rather crudely made from nodules of weathered chert and flint, though some beautiful hollow-based arrowheads from the period have been found. Rectangular and oval palettes were fashioned from slate and porphyry, and some small vases were carved from basalt. Small copper tools and pins have been found in graves, but the use of metals was rare. Large quantities of beads made from steatite, jasper, and carnelian from the Eastern and Western Deserts, as well as shells from the Red Sea, were strung together for necklaces and belts. Pottery and goods of ivory, stone, and metal were commonly offered as funerary gifts in the characteristically oval or roughly circular Badarian pit graves.[2]

The large variety and quantities of raw materials seem to indicate that the Badarians were involved in a well-developed trade network. Most of the materials were probably obtained from the Western or Eastern Desert, but some, such as ivory and porphyry, may have come from Nubia;[3] turquoise and copper may have been acquired from the Sinai or Palestine.[4] At least indirect contact with Palestine is suggested by the discovery of a loop-handled Palestinian jar found at Badari.[5]

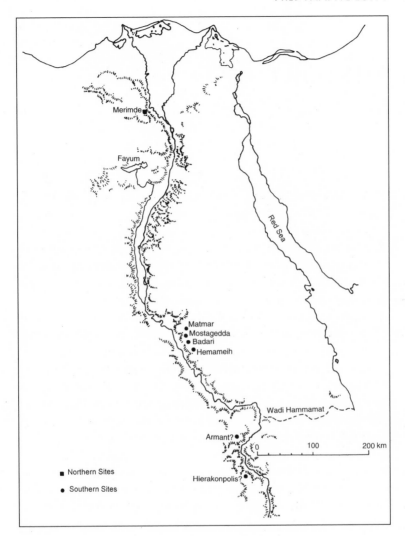

Fig. 4. Egypt, ca. 5000–4000 B.C.

Roughly contemporary with the Badarian culture of Upper Egypt was the Fayum A culture of Lower Egypt (fig. 4).[6] The people who inhabited the Fayum region at that time manufactured the type of fine, hollow-based arrowheads that have also been found on Badarian sites.[7] Their pottery, on the other hand, is rather plain and was fired at low temperatures.[8] These people depended on some domesticated plants and animals, such as emmer wheat, barley, pigs, and goats,[9] but a large part of their diet consisted of fish, wild fowl, and game animals.[10] They also hunted hippopotamus and elephant, and harvested ivory, but as there is an absence of evidence to suggest that they actually worked the ivory, it may have been collected purely for trade, possibly for turquoise, amazonite, and shells from the Mediterranean and Red Seas.[11] Luxury goods are rare, consisting of small palettes, stone beads, and a few stone bowls. Overall, the Fayum A culture was much simpler than its Badarian counterpart.[12]

The people of Merimde (ca. 5000–4000 B.C.), who lived on the southwest edge of the Delta (fig. 4),[13] were similar to those of the Fayum A culture. These farming and pastoral people made small palettes, stone bowls, and also fine hollow-based arrowheads that are similar to those at Badarian and Fayum A sites, and like the people of Fayum A they did not bury funerary offerings with their dead.[14] The site of Merimde, however, is larger and appears to have been more prosperous than the site of Fayum A; its inhabitants used a wider variety of tools, made of a wider variety of materials, than did the people of the Fayum A culture.

Approximately midway through the fifth millennium, the Ghassulian culture, one with extensive trade connections, appears in Palestine (ca. 4500–3300 B.C.).[15] The Ghassulians obtained hematite and turquoise from the Sinai; basalt from the Golan Heights; obsidian from Anatolia;[16] possibly arsenical copper from Anatolia, Iran, or the Caucasus mountains;[17] shells from the Red Sea and the Nile; and elephant tusks from either Egypt or North Syria.[18]

Evidence for contact among the cultures of these various areas have been found. Pear-shaped and spheroid maceheads,[19] ladles, and footed containers appear at Ghassulian sites and at Merimde.[20] A few pottery vessels with pierced lug handles and a few ladles similar to those from Merimde and Ghassulian sites have been discovered at Hemamieh and Mostagedda in Upper Egypt.[21] Ghassulian and Badarian ivory carvings also show similarities.[22] Finally, some pottery types,[23] metallurgical technology,[24] wall paintings,[25] and maceheads seem to indicate links between the Ghassulian and Mesopotamian cultures.[26] Even at this early date, therefore, we may see the beginnings of regional trade activities that indirectly connected northern Mesopotamia with Egypt.

The Badarian period is succeeded in Upper Egypt by the Naqada I or Amratian period (ca. 4000–3500 B.C.). Naqada I sites extend from Hierakonpolis in the south to as far north as Matmar (fig. 5), with Naqada I influence perhaps felt as far south as Qustul in Nubia

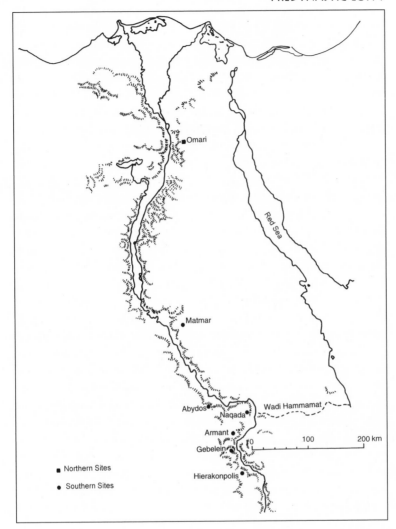

Fig. 5. Egypt, ca. 4000–3750 B.C.

(fig. 1).[27] Egyptian slate palettes, combs, hairpins, and pottery dating to the end of the Naqada I period and the beginning of the Naqada II period have been found in early A-Group graves in Lower Nubia (fig. 5).[28]

Naqada I sites appear larger and seem to have been wealthier than Badarian ones. The increased diversity and quality of artifacts suggests the development of a complex division of labor that culminates with the first evidence of mud-brick houses and fortifications

at the end of the period. The greater wealth of the Naqada I culture
is also reflected in the quality and number of grave goods found in
some burials, even though we see at the same time a greater disparity
in the wealth of grave offerings; a large number of graves exhibit only
one pot interred with the body.[29]

The Naqada I culture, like the Badarian culture before it, does
not seem to have been strongly influenced by its neighbors, but this
situation may be more apparent than real. Egyptian sherds assigned
to the Naqada I period have been found at a chalcolithic site in
northeastern Sinai.[30] Further, it is possible that the technique of making faience came to Egypt from Mesopotamia at this time.[31]

The Omari A culture in Lower Egypt (ca. 4000–3750 B.C.) is
roughly contemporary with the first half of the Naqada I period (fig.
5).[32] Among the flint implements are many types common to both
the Fayum A and Merimde cultures, although this much larger variety of stone tools foreshadows the stone industry of the later Maadi
culture. Likewise, the pottery bears a resemblance to that of the other
two cultures, and, as during the preceding periods, it has nothing in
common with Upper Egyptian pottery. The people of Omari A grew
foddervetch similar to that grown at Merimde, but emmer wheat is
the most common grain found at the site. These cereals were probably used to make bread. Fish bones are the most plentiful, but pig,
cattle, goat, sheep, and donkey bones have also been recovered, suggesting that this group depended on fishing and domesticated animals for their subsistence. Crocodile, hippopotamus, and tortoise
remains indicate some hunting. There is no evidence for the use of
metal, but a pot containing approximately 15 kilograms of galena
suggest that if metals were not worked, they were collected for trade.
Finally, in contrast with the rich Naqada I burials, little or nothing
was buried with the dead.[33]

The Maadi culture (ca. 3750–3200 B.C.) succeeded the Omari A
culture in Lower Egypt,[34] spanning the last half of the Naqada I period and possibly the Naqada IIc period in Egypt, and from the Late
Chalcolithic until sometime during the Early Bronze Ia period in
Palestine. Unlike earlier Lower Egyptian cultures, it is quite widespread, reaching from Buto in the north to Sedment in the south (fig.
6). Contacts with the Naqada I and Naqada IIa/b cultures are manifest
in the appearance of rhombic slate palettes, disc-shaped maceheads,
jars made of diorite, possibly some flint tools, and black-topped pottery. Maadi peoples tried to copy this Upper Egyptian pottery but were

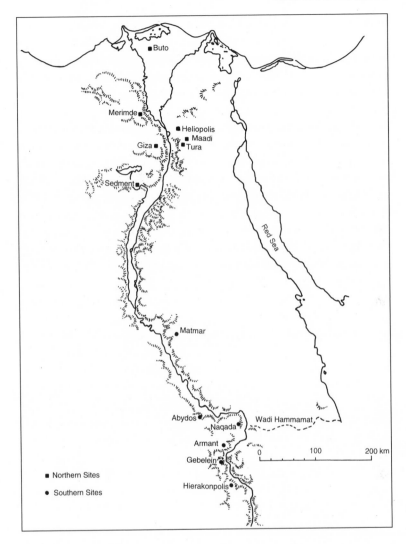

Fig. 6. Egypt, ca. 3750–3200 B.C.

never able to perfect the firing technique that produced its shiny black top. From Palestine, they imported jars, V-shaped bowls, basalt rings, tabular scrapers, blades of flint, and asphalt. Most of the large Palestinian vessels were seemingly imported as containers, however, rather than for any intrinsic value, as there was no attempt by the Maadians to copy them. In turn, Maadian exports of Lower Egyptian black ware, flints, pectoral fin spikes from the Nile catfish, and shells, especially of the *Aspatharia* (Spathopsis) *rubens caillaudi*, have been found at Site H at Wadi Ghazzeh in southern Palestine. Moreover, four underground structures at Maadi are similar to those found at the chalcolithic site at Beersheba, and they may have been homes of Palestinian traders. Based on the archaeological evidence, then, the Maadians appear to have had much stronger trade ties with Palestine than with Upper Egypt (fig. 7).[35]

The Naqada I period is followed by the Naqada II or Gerzean period, which can be divided into an early (ca. 3500–3300 B.C.) and a late phase (ca. 3300–3200 B.C.). The distribution of Naqada IIa/b sites is similar to that of the Naqada I period (fig. 6). The quantity and quality of ivory, stone, ceramic, and metal artifacts from Naqada II sites and graves indicate a society that enjoyed greater wealth, population, technical innovation, division of labor, and social stratification than earlier Egyptian cultures. The best evidence of this wealth and social stratification comes from burials. Most were similar to

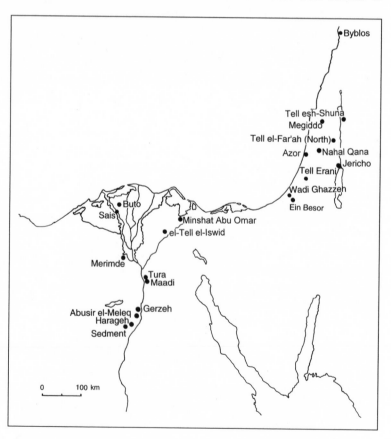

Fig. 7. Egyptian and Palestinian Sites

those of the Naqada I period, with the dead interred in shallow oval or rectangular pits with a modest number of burial offerings. A minority, on the other hand, were large rectangular pits, containing rich offerings, approximately three meters deep with reinforced roofs and walls. By the end of the Naqada II period, the burials for the elite had evolved into larger brick-lined chambers, some with more than one room and even richer offerings.[36]

During the Naqada IIc/d period, the Maadi settlements, except for Buto, disappeared and were replaced by others reflecting Upper Egyptian culture at Sedment, Harageh, and Abusir el Meleq in southern Lower Egypt and Minshat Abu Omar in the eastern Delta (fig. 8). Buto appears to have survived until the end of the Naqada III period,[37] yet after Naqada II sites had become established in the eastern Delta it experienced a transitional period during which local Lower Egyptian pottery was slowly replaced by Upper Egyptian pottery. This transition occurred before the unification of Egypt.

Thomas von der Way explains this transition by speculating that a chieftain from Upper Egypt seized control of Lower Egypt, but, because of the presumed importance of Buto, killed only the ruling class, after which the commoners were slowly assimilated into the new culture. The Narmer palette, von der Way contends, may depict the conquest of this last Naqada chiefdom.[38] Considering that pottery is only one aspect of a culture, it is possible that this transition period at Buto may be nothing more than an indication of the strong influence of Upper Egyptian culture in the North and of Buto's access to new pottery-making techniques after the establishment of Naqada IIc/d sites such as Minshat Abu Omar in the Delta. As previously mentioned, there were attempts at Maadi to imitate Upper Egyptian pottery.

The expansion of Naqada IIc/d settlements into Lower Egypt may have coincided with an increased Egyptian presence in the northern Sinai[39] and southern Palestine.[40] This presence presaged a second and even larger growth of Egyptian influence in the same two areas[41] that appears to correspond with the unification of Egypt. Yet, even at the height of its influence in Palestine, Egypt's predynastic presence there was confined to the south, primarily around the three sites of Ain Besor, Tel Erani,[42] and Azor (fig. 7).[43] Egyptian influence did extend farther north to Megiddo and nearby sites, but most artifacts found there are of local types.[44] Therefore, during the Naqada II period, any land trade conducted by Egypt with Mesopotamia

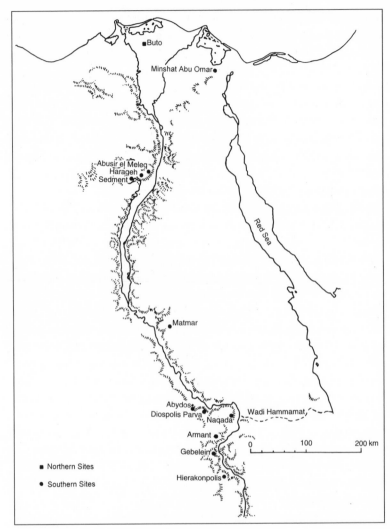

Fig. 8. Egypt, ca.
3200–3100 B.C.

through Palestine was almost surely indirect. This is important to note because it is in the Naqada IIc/d period that we find the strongest evidence of Mesopotamian influences in Egypt. Pottery styles, motifs, and cylinder seals similar to those found in Mesopotamia now appear in Upper Egypt.[45]

As Egyptian influence spread to the north, it apparently mirrored the situation in the south. Although no evidence for Naqada II settlements exists in Lower Nubia, a steady increase in Upper Egyptian influence there through the Naqada II and Naqada III periods continued into the beginning of the First Dynasty. This influence is demonstrated by a large number of Egyptian artifacts found in early and classical A-Group graves.[46] In the same period, native Nubian ware (N-ware) was placed in Naqada II graves, and Nubian pottery discovered in burials increased in frequency throughout the Naqada III period and early in the First Dynasty.[47]

The last period is the Naqada III, or Dynasty O (3200–3100 B.C.). At the beginning, the new power of regional kings is seen in the appearance of true royal cemeteries, as at Abydos, and possibly a trend in some areas toward the concentration of the populace around administrative centers, such as Hierakonpolis. The period is best known for its carved ivory knife handles and large ceremonial slate palettes that bear both scenes of war and Mesopotamian motifs. It is a time of transition that culminates with the rise of a true Egyptian state.[48] It has been argued that Egypt was unified as early as the Naqada IIIa period under a King Scorpion. This interpretation is based on a number of artifacts and royal symbols recovered from Tomb U-j at Abydos. These artifacts consist of an ivory scepter in the shape of a crook, Palestinian pottery, and bone or ivory labels possibly attached to bolts of cloth, of which one was decorated with a palace-facade motif.[49] The evidence that this early king ruled over a unified Egypt consists of a few bone labels that may be inscribed with the name of Buto or Bubastis. These labels may be evidence of raiding or trade, but they hardly constitute evidence of a unified country. This tomb undoubtedly housed the remains of an early king, but whether it was a regional king or a king that may have ruled as far north as Minshat Abu Omar is unknown. A political unification is still best marked by the rise of the Egyptian state at the beginning of the First Dynasty.

As previously mentioned, Egyptian ties with Palestine and Nubia continued to grow during the Naqada III period and into the First Dynasty, but the nature of relations with Mesopotamia at this time is more difficult to discern. A review of Mesopotamian artifacts and motifs may help clarify this issue.

4

THE POTTERY

Three types of Egyptian pottery dating to the Naqada II period appear to be derived from Mesopotamian prototypes: loop-handled containers, tubular-spouted vessels, and triangular-lugged vessels.[1]

Loop-handled containers are found in Mesopotamia from the Ubaid period through the Jamdat Nasr period, but in Anatolia, Lebanon, and Palestine they are not known before the Uruk and Jamdat Nasr periods,[2] nor in Egypt before the Naqada II period.[3] Because such containers did not evolve from local wares in Palestine and Egypt,[4] and because some of their earliest examples have been unearthed in Cilicia,[5] their distribution throughout western Asia makes it likely that at least some types came to Egypt from the north through Palestine (fig. 9).

One loop-handled container used as evidence for trade between northern Syria and Egypt via Palestine is a small jug with vertical stripes from Jericho. This jug is closely paralleled by one found at Gerzeh in Egypt,[6] and by another recovered from a late chalcolithic tomb at Tarsus, in Cilicia (see respectively, figs. 10A, B, and C).[7] The jug from Jericho has a small ridge slightly below its mouth. This ridge is absent on the examples from Egypt and Tarsus. The jugs from Gerzeh and Tarsus are painted with stripes that extend from their mouths to their bases. In contrast, the jug from Jericho exhibits painted stripes that extend from its mouth down to a horizontal stripe painted above its base. The handle on this container is also painted whereas those of the other two are not. The greater similarity of the jugs from Tarsus and Egypt to one another therefore suggests that this type of loop-handled container did not necessarily reach Egypt via Palestine but may have come directly from Cilicia.

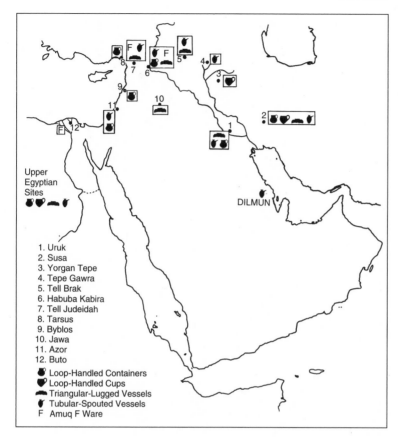

Fig. 9. *Distribution*
of Pottery

A specific type of loop-handled container consists of a cup whose earliest examples in Egypt come from Mostagedda, Diospolis Parva, and Badari. Their dates, however, are not secure (see respectively, figs. 11A, B, and C). The cup from Mostagedda was a surface find. That from Diospolis Parva is illustrated but is not even mentioned in the excavation reports. The cup from Badari is the most securely dated, having been discovered in a dump with eight pots that are assigned to the end of Naqada IIb through Naqada IId.[8] Such cups were originally believed to be Palestinian,[9] but the evidence to support this claim comprises fragments of Palestinian loop-handled jars and pitchers from Palestine, both with pronounced and constricted necks, rather than actual cups.

Only two close parallels exist for the loop-handled cups, one from Yorgan Tepe and the other from Susa (figs. 11D and E).[10] The

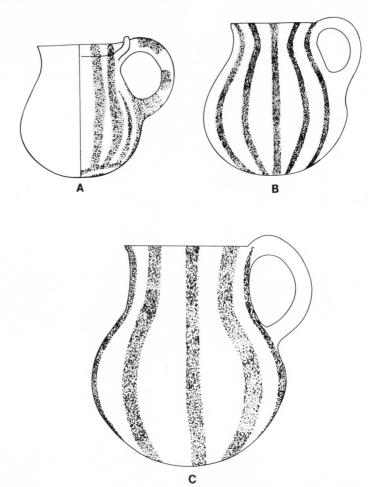

Fig. 10. Loop-Handled Jugs: A. Jericho, B. Gerzeh, and C. Tarsus. (After Hennessey 1967: pl. 19.1–3)

cup from Mostagedda is similar to that from Yorgan Tepe, both in shape and in red slip. These cups suggest a trade route around Palestine, from which cups are absent (fig. 9).

Containers with tubular spouts were very common in Mesopotamia during the Uruk and Jamdat Nasr periods in the south and the Gawra period in the north.[11] They appear in Palestine during the later part of the Chalcolithic period and continue through Early Bronze I. In Egypt, locally made spouted wares are found throughout the Naqada II period (figs. 12A, B and C).[12] The Egyptian containers show stronger affinities to those from Mesopotamia during the Late Uruk period than to the spouted containers from Palestine (see re-

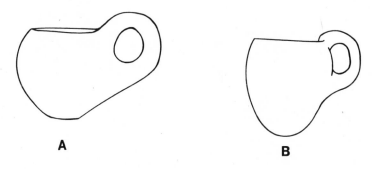

A **B**

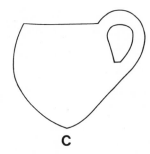

C

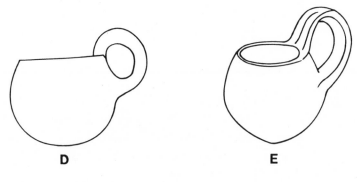

D **E**

Fig. 11. Loop-Handled Cups: A. Mostagedda, B. Diospolis Parva, C. Badari, D. Yorgan Tepe, and E. Susa. (After Brunton and Caton-Thompson 1928: pls. 46.12, 47.2; Brunton 1937: pls. 34.19, 32.2; Petrie 1901a: pl. 19.70; Starr 1937: pl. 41 O; Mecquenem 1928: fig. 2)

A

B

C

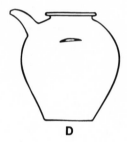

D

*Fig. 12. Tubular-
Spouted Vessels:
A–B. Naqada,
C. Badari, D. Ras el
Ain, and E–F.
Uruk, (After Kan-
tor 1965: fig. 4
M–P, U, T)*

E

F

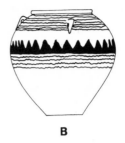

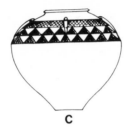

Fig. 13.
Triangular-Lugged
Vessels: A–B. Na-
qada, and C. Susa,
(After Petrie 1915:
pl. 35.59C, 35.59P;
Breton 1957: fig.
14.9)

spectively, figs. 12E, F, and D),[13] which suggests that Egypt's contacts with the north, perhaps even Tell Judeidah in the Amuq valley,[14] were direct and did not involve Palestine.

Triangular-lugged vessels first appeared in Mesopotamia during the Ubaid period and became increasingly common during the Late Uruk and Jamdat Nasr periods. Helene Kantor doubts that early triangular-lugged pottery in Egypt was derived from such vessels because of morphological differences,[15] yet for two reasons, a Mesopotamian origin for these triangular lugs is likely. First, triangular lugs are quite distinctive, and second, triangular-lugged pottery appears in Egypt at the same time that tubular-spouted jars do (fig. 13).

There are in Egypt, however, three pots with triangular lugs that Kantor believes are direct Mesopotamian imports (compare figs. 14 and 15). These pots date to the Naqada IIc/d period and seem to be contemporary with the appearance of the Mesopotamian "colonies" in northern Syria. One of these sites, Habuba Kabira, is known for its pottery production, and vessels with triangular lugs are plentiful

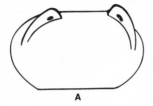
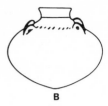

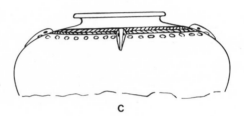

Fig. 14. Mesopota-
mian Imports?:
A. Matmar, B. Mos-
tagedda, C. Badari,
(After Brunton
1948: pl. 12.22;
Brunton 1937: pl.
35.24; Brunton and
Caton-Thompson
1928: pl.
40.D59W)

there.[16] Similar vessels with triangular lugs have been found at Jawa in northern Lebanon, which appears to have been the southern extent of this type of pottery in the region (fig. 9).[17] Triangular-lugged pottery also appears at Tell Judeidah (fig. 9).[18] In light of the proximity of Habuba Kabira and Tell Judeidah to the sea, the existence of a sea route linking northern Syria to northern Egypt is plausible. This proposal is supported by the fact that triangular-lugged pottery, tubular-spouted pottery, and the multiple-brush technique of painting pottery all appeared in Egypt at approximately the same time.[19] Multiple-brush painting spread from Iran through northern Mesopotamia to places such as Tell Judeidah and Hama in the west,[20] and, like the triangular-lugged pottery, it is absent from Palestine, which further supports the possibility of a sea route that bypassed Palestine.

Fragments of two other vessel types may also connect Habuba Kabira with Egypt and Palestine. According to Dietrich Sürenhagen, a Palestinian ledge handle believed to date to the Late Chalcolithic period and a rim fragment that is thought to be a type of Nubian ware from the Naqada IIc period have been found at Habuba Kab-

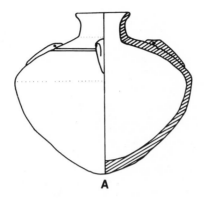

A

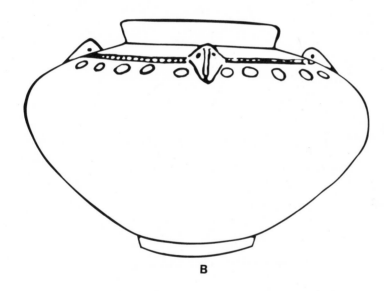

B

*Fig. 15.
Triangular-Lugged
Vessels from Mesopo-
tamia: A. Habuba
Kabira, and B. Tel-
loh. (After Sürenha-
gen 1977: pl.
18.124; Genouillac
1934: pl. 25.2)*

ira.[21] The use of a sea route is supported by the discovery of Amuq F
chaff-faced ware at the Deltaic site of Buto.[22] This ware is common
at Tell Judeidah, and local vessels made of it are found at Habuba
Kabira (fig. 9).[23]

Of the types of containers just discussed, only that with a tubular
spout is found in the Persian Gulf region during the Uruk period. In
fact, the one fragment of probable Uruk pottery known from the

region is a spout from just such a container. The only other artifact found that can be firmly dated to the Uruk period is a *bulla*. The only Jamdat Nasr-type pottery found there is a biconical pot with everted rim and geometric designs painted in black, white, and plum around the shoulder. This pottery was made from the beginning of the Jamdat Nasr period to the end of the early dynastic era in southern Mesopotamia;[24] however, there are no known parallels in Egypt dating to the Naqada II period or any subsequent period.

It is possible to reconstruct from the archaeological evidence a land route that leads from Mesopotamia through northern Syria, Palestine, and finally to Egypt. I believe, however, that the evidence presented above points instead to a sea route linking Egypt with northern Syria at least by the Naqada IIc/d period and probably earlier. In contrast, it is not possible to reconstruct a southern route linking Egypt with the Persian Gulf. A review of raw materials may clarify the situation.

RAW MATERIALS

5

Upper Egypt, with an abundant supply of various stones and some metals, was able to satisfy most of its needs for raw materials during the Predynastic period.[1]

Copper in the form of malachite and native copper was probably acquired from the Eastern Desert,[2] though copper ore and some cast-copper objects dating to the Naqada II period may have been imported from Palestine via Lower Egypt.[3]

Timber has been considered an import from Syria during predynastic times, but, according to Alessandra Nibbi and Alfred Lucas, there is little foundation for such a belief.[4] Karl Butzer argues convincingly for a moister climate that may have produced an environment conducive to the growing of many of the various types of trees used in Egypt during this period.[5]

Obsidian is commonly found in western Asia from as early as the Neolithic period. It was intermittently imported into Palestine, Mesopotamia, and the Persian Gulf region from ca. 5000 to 2300 B.C. (fig. 16); Egypt imported it during the Naqada II period, even perhaps as early as the Naqada I period. The obsidian found at Upper Egyptian sites appears to have come from the coasts of present-day Yemen and Eritrea, though whether it came via the Red Sea or partly overland and down the Nile we do not know. Recent analysis of an obsidian tool from the Deltaic site of el-Tell el-Iswid (south), on the other hand, suggests that it came from Nemrut Dağ in Anatolia (figs. 7, 16).[6]

Syro-Palestinian settlements acquired their obsidian from Äci-gol and Çiftlik in Anatolia—perhaps it made its way south in the same manner as did some of the pottery, such as some loop-handled

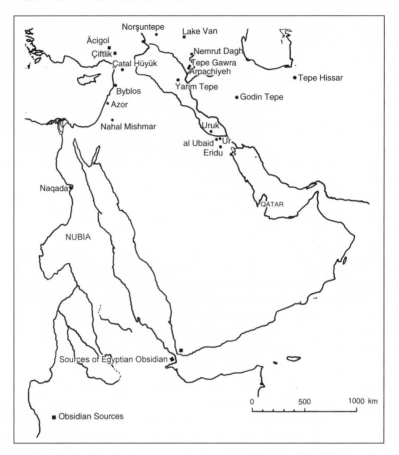

Fig. 16. Obsidian Sources of Raw Materials

containers, mentioned in the previous chapter—but Mesopotamian and eastern Arabian sites obtained Anatolian obsidian from the Lake Van and Nemrut Dağ areas (fig. 16). Obsidian recovered in Qatar, from a grave dated to the Ubaid period, appears to come from southwestern Arabia, whether via a land or a sea route, we do not know,[7] but the subpluvial phase that took place for part of the Ubaid period would have been more conducive to trade via land routes than in other times.

At least twenty-three silver artifacts dating to the Late Predynastic period have been found in Egypt, but there is considerable disagreement concerning their origin. For example, Lucas has concluded, based on the analyses of eighteen artifacts, that the silver objects dating to this period were probably fashioned from a local aurian silver, a natural silver-rich gold ore.[8] More recent analyses by N. H. Gale and Z. A. Stos-Gale suggest that two types of silver were used to make artifacts in Egypt prior to the Middle Kingdom. One type consists of 5 percent or less of gold and is believed to have been extracted from argentiferous galena or argentiferous cerussite. A characteristic of this refining process is that silver from such ores will have between 0.01 to 1 percent of lead and rarely up to 2.5 percent;[9] all silver samples tested by Gale and Stos-Gale with low percentages of gold have small amounts of lead, suggesting that these artifacts are made from smelted silver. They argue, however, since most galena deposits in Egypt contain too little silver to be exploited, and since a comparison of lead-isotope analyses of galena ores and artifacts containing lead lack similarities, it appears that this refined silver came from ores mined and processed outside of Egypt. The second type of silver contains more than 20 percent gold and is believed to come from aurian silver as Lucas proposes. Similar samples from modern Egyptian gold mines were reported by C. J. Alford in 1900, and analyses of silver artifacts with a high percentage of gold consistently lack lead, which indicates that this type of silver was not extracted from galena or cerussite, but, instead, came from ores that contain aurian silver.[10]

This interpretation has been challenged by G. Philip and T. Rehren. They point out that aurian silver is very rare and would most likely appear in ores that are very difficult to process, and that the original data cited by Alford in his report on aurian-silver samples are now missing and cannot be verified; they then dismiss this report without discussing its merits. Philip and Rehren argue, instead, that this "aurian silver" did not come from a silver-rich gold but results from the indiscriminate mixing of metals when gold and silver objects are melted down in preparation for recasting. They believe that all silver found in Egypt is silver cupellated from lead and was acquired through trade.[11] One difficulty with this theory of mixing metals is that it does not explain why silver artifacts containing 5 to 20 percent gold are so rare in Egypt prior to the Middle Kingdom. We would expect a more random distribution of gold content when metals are mixed as Philip and Rehren describe. Another difficulty is that we would expect objects made of different metals to be sorted by metal type before being melted down because some metals are far more valuable than others, and it is unlikely that rarer metals would be added as a minor constituent of more common metals. For example, outside of Egypt native silver is 20 percent as abundant as gold, and when we consider that most of the silver found at this time is not native silver but smelted silver, it suggests that silver is relatively common in comparison to gold. Therefore, when small amounts of gold are melted down with silver, the gold is in effect sacrificed to increase the supplies of silver. Under these conditions, it appears more likely that silver and copper would be added to gold.

In contrast, at the beginning of the First Dynasty in Egypt, one part of gold was valued at two and one-half parts of silver, and silver continued to be rarer than gold until the Middle Kingdom.[12] If Philip and Rehren are correct that silver in Egypt was imported, it is possible that the Egyptians were adding the more common gold and copper to silver to increase their supplies of silver. But considering that silver alloys either have less than 5 percent gold or more than 20 percent gold signifies a more deliberate alloying procedure than that proposed by Philip and Rehren.

Two other flaws are evident in Philip and Rehren's study. Their study, like that of Gale and Stos-Gale, lacks the necessary geologic data from Egypt and Anatolia to support their arguments, and both studies rely too heavily on data from other regions. As R. W. Boyle points out, the amount of silver present in gold-bearing ores will not only vary considerably from one region to the next but also even within the same vein. In some Precambrian ores the early pyrites will be rich in silver and later pyrites will lack silver, but in Mesozoic-Cenozoic deposits the opposite trend is seen. Depth and heat can also affect the fineness of a vein because silver migrates away from heat. Therefore, the deeper gold veins near a hot spot or veins cut by dykes will have little or no silver, while sections away from heat sources will be enriched. Even in relatively small areas the fineness of gold can vary considerably in the same deposits.[13] So, more geologic data are needed from the areas being discussed before any definitive statements can be made concerning the origin of aurian silver in Egypt.

The second flaw with their theory that smelted silver was used instead of aurian silver is that they fail to explain the lack of lead in these gold-rich alloys. As previously mentioned, lead is always found in silver refined from galena, but we do not find lead in the "aurian silver" from Egypt. This lack of lead may be owing to the fact that if gold or copper is present at greater than 10 to 15 percent, lead may be insensitive to the X-ray fluorescence analyses used by Gale and

Stos-Gale,[14] but lead was absent in most of the samples reported earlier by Lucas, which supports Gale and Stos-Gale's results.[15] Until a more detailed study of the lead content in these early silver artifacts is undertaken our questions concerning the origin of aurian silver in Egypt must remain unanswered. We can only state that silver alloys with a high percentage of gold and copper come from Egypt as early as the Predynastic period.

Since Gale and Stos-Gale published their findings on early silver in Egypt more extensive analyses of galena ores have been undertaken by A. A. Hassan and F. A. Hassan. Hassan and Hassan insist that the isotopic composition of lead from some silver artifacts is similar to that found in galena deposits located near the Red Sea. Therefore, it is not necessary to look beyond the Eastern Desert of Egypt to find the types of ores needed to produce the silver used during the Predynastic period.[16] But even if the ancient Egyptians did extract silver from galena, the rarity of silver in Egypt before the Middle Kingdom suggests that, at most, only small amounts of silver were being recovered by this method, and Egypt was probably forced to acquire some silver through trade.

The largest group of silver objects (>233) was discovered outside of Egypt in a cemetery of the *énéolithique* period (ca. 3800–3200 B.C.) at Byblos, but most of the graves containing silver at Byblos are believed to date to ca. 3500–3200 B.C. South of Byblos, the *énéolithique* level at Tell el-Far'ah has yielded a silver bowl, and at Azor six silver earrings of late predynastic date (ca. 3100 B.C.) were found,[17] and a fragment of sheet silver, dating to the last few centuries of the fourth millennium, was discovered at Tell esh-Shuna (fig. 7).[18] To the east silver jewelry from level IIA at Tepe Hissar (ca. 3800 B.C.)[19] in northwestern Iran appears to be contemporary with the silver jewelry discovered at Byblos.[20] In Susa and southern Mesopotamia the earliest silver artifacts date to the Late Uruk period, and only a few silver artifacts have survived from this time.[21]

According to Kay Prag, the concentration of silver objects at Byblos suggests that it was an important trading center between Egypt and Anatolia. Prag's supposition of trade with Anatolia is based on several phenomena at Byblos. Grave offerings of jewelry, maceheads, and daggers, for example, and successive multiple burials in pithoi have affinity with both regions; further, the copper and silver found at Byblos may have come from an Anatolian source.[22] There is, however, a flaw in this theory. The earliest silver artifacts from Anatolia all date to ca. 3000 B.C., too late to qualify it as the source of the Biblite silver.[23] In a later article, Prag reverses herself and suggests that silver found at Byblos was from Egypt. This theory is also flawed. The type of silver found at Byblos and Azor is of a high purity and is free of gold. If it came from Egypt, it must have been extracted from local galena or cerussite, but Prag admits it is unlikely that the Egyptians had developed the cupellation methods necessary to produce such silver at this early date.[24]

Any discussion of the origins of silver metallurgy in the Near East must recognize the interval between the initial appearances of lead and silver. Lead is obtained by smelting galena or cerussite, and silver is obtained primarily through the cupellation of lead. The development of the latter process probably occurred over a long time, because many technical problems must have been solved before the silver could be extracted efficiently. We would therefore expect to find lead artifacts long before the appearance of silver,[25] and this is in fact the case. The earliest lead object comes from Çatal Hüyük (seventh millennium) and is followed by one from Yarim Tepe and one from Tell Sotto (sixth millennium), one from Arpachiyeh (fifth millennium), what may be a lead strip from an *énéolithique* grave at Byblos,[26] and lead seems to have appeared in Palestine at about the same time it did in Byblos.

As mentioned in chapter 3, it has been proposed that arsenical copper was imported from Anatolia, Iran, or the Caucasus Mountains by the Ghassulian peoples of Palestine. A cache of 429 arsenical copper objects dating to ca. 3500 B.C. were discovered in a cave high on the north bank of Nahal Mishmar (fig. 16).[27] Some of the items were found to have a high lead content that may be due to the addition of metallic lead; lead had also been used to repair casting defects to several of these artifacts.[28] Thus, the significant amount of lead lends credence to the theory that arsenical copper or metallurgical techniques were being imported into Palestine during the Ghassulian period. Recently, M. Tadmor and M. Gates in separate studies of the typology and metallurgic techniques of these copper artifacts raised the possibility that this hoard was cached by traders,[29] which supports the possibility that copper and lead or metallurgical techniques were imported.

The only lead artifact attributed to predynastic Egypt is a hawk model from Upper Egypt dating to the Naqada IIc period. Initially, because of the high silver content of the lead and its lead isotope signature, N. H. Gale and Z. A. Stos-Gale concluded that the lead must have been imported.[30] More recent X-ray fluorescence analysis shows that this model lacks silver and is almost pure lead; chemical and lead isotope analyses imply a common origin with an aurian-silver vessel rim (Naqada IId) from Upper Egypt.[31] The similarity of the lead in the hawk to galena near the Red Sea suggests a possible Egyptian origin for this model. It should also be noted that the rarity of lead in Egypt during the Predynastic period argues against the possibility that substantial amounts of silver were being extracted from galena at this time.

The sudden appearance of lead and smelted silver in Egypt, the late date at which both appear (Naqada II), and the appearance of Mesopotamian influences during the same period suggest that either refined silver or the technique of extracting silver from argentiferous ores was brought to Egypt from Anatolia or northern Syria. The early appearance of lead in Anatolia, the distribution pattern of lead artifacts ranging from Egypt to Anatolia, the paucity of silver and lead in southern Mesopotamia, Iran, and Egypt, the large amount of silver at Byblos, and the discovery of an elaborate metallurgy industry at Norşuntepe, which is located in a region rich in silver, all support Prag's original conclusion that southern Anatolia was a center of silver production (figs. 16, 17). The primary objection to this proposal is the absence of cupellated-silver artifacts in Anatolia until after smelted silver appears at Byblos, but more recent evidence indicating that the process of cupellating silver from lead was being utilized at Habuba Kabira may nullify this objection and supports Prag's original conclusion.[32]

Although the silver and lead discussed above have uncertain origins, the evidence suggests that silver was being produced in Anatolia or northern Syria and being exported to the south. It also appears that aurian silver was being mined or was being produced as an artificial alloy in Egypt. The rather sudden appearance and distribution of both silver and lead throughout the Near East seems to indicate a trade route passing through northern Mesopotamia and northern Syria down the coast of Syro-Palestine to Egypt. As noted earlier, at the same time that silver is being imported to Byblos it makes its first appearance at Tepe Hissar (level IIA) in northern Iran, precisely when lapis lazuli also makes its first appearance there.[33]

Lapis lazuli is important because Badakhshan in Afghanistan is its only known source at this time. Thus, it had to come to Egypt via

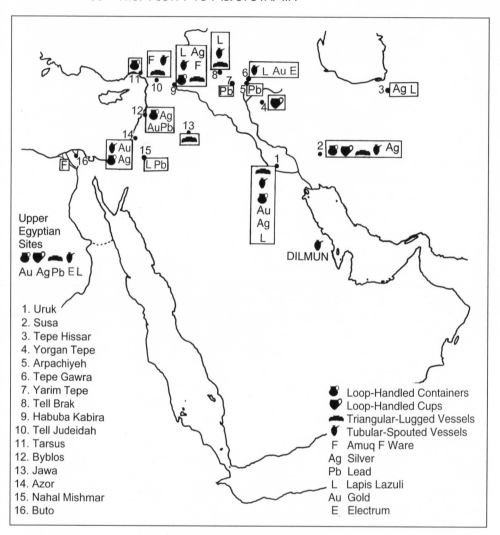

Upper
Egyptian
Sites

Au Ag Pb E L

1. Uruk
2. Susa
3. Tepe Hissar
4. Yorgan Tepe
5. Arpachiyeh
6. Tepe Gawra
7. Yarim Tepe
8. Tell Brak
9. Habuba Kabira
10. Tell Judeidah
11. Tarsus
12. Byblos
13. Jawa
14. Azor
15. Nahal Mishmar
16. Buto

DILMUN

Loop-Handled Containers
Loop-Handled Cups
Triangular-Lugged Vessels
Tubular-Spouted Vessels
F Amuq F Ware
Ag Silver
Pb Lead
L Lapis Lazuli
Au Gold
E Electrum

Fig. 17. Distribution of Raw Materials   Mesopotamia. It first appears in Egypt during the Naqada IIa/b period (ca. 3500–3300 B.C.), but only in the Naqada IIc/d period (ca. 3300–3200 B.C.) does it become relatively common.[34] Lapis lazuli beads possibly dating to the end of the Chalcolithic period (ca. 3500–3300 B.C.) have been found in southern Palestine at Nahal Mishmar, near the cache of arsenical copper artifacts discussed above (fig. 16).[35]

Lapis lazuli is important to this study because in Egyptian graves it is usually found in association with other foreign elements,[36] which raises the possibility that they arrived via the same route. This semiprecious stone may have appeared in northern Mesopotamia as early as the end of the Ubaid period (Gawra XIII, ca. 4000 B.C.), but it is rare and this date is not secure. It continues to be rare until level X (3500 B.C.) at which time it is abundant,[37] but, with the exception of one bead from Uruk dating to the end of the Late Uruk period,[38] it does not appear at southern Mesopotamian sites until the Jamdat Nasr period (ca. 3100 B.C.) and is not found around the Persian Gulf until the Early Dynastic II period (ca. 2700 B.C.).[39] Therefore, if the date is correct for the beads from Palestine, and because lapis lazuli is found at northern Mesopotamian sites during the Naqada IIa/b period in Egypt, it is possible that Egypt received its earliest supplies of lapis lazuli from northern Mesopotamia via a land route through Palestine. The evidence for such a route is supported by the fact that faience beads were also discovered with the lapis lazuli beads in what may have been a trader's cave at Nahal Mishmar.[40] This appears to be the earliest evidence for faience in Palestine and roughly coincides with the appearance of faience in Egypt.[41] Also, with the exception of Egypt and Nahal Mishmar in Palestine, Tepe Gawra is the only known site from this period with both lapis lazuli and faience.[42] It is also possible that lapis lazuli and faience came to Palestine via Egypt.

The Naqada IIc/d period, when lapis lazuli becomes abundant in Egypt, seems to coincide with the appearance of Mesopotamian "colonies" in northern Syria, a sharp decline of lapis lazuli and gold in level IX at Tepe Gawra, and an absence of lapis lazuli in Palestine. Thus, it appears that at this later time the most likely route between the two areas would be through northern Syria and then by sea to Egypt (fig. 17). This is supported by the discovery of a few pieces of unworked lapis lazuli at the Mesopotamian colony of Jebel Aruda in northern Syria.[43]

A small lapis lazuli figurine, however, is used to lend credence to the possibility of a sea route between the Persian Gulf and Egypt. The figurine comes from Hierakonpolis and dates to the end of the Predynastic period (fig 18).[44] Edith Porada points out a number of physical similarities between this figurine and figurines from Mesopotamia, but she believes that such details as the shape and positioning of breasts and buttocks vary so much as to prohibit the establishment of valid parallels. She does believe that the crossed hands on the figurine are important, and that the closest parallels for this gesture are to be found on Iranian figurines. These figurines, however, are dated to the later part of the second millennium B.C.,

Fig. 18. Lapis Lazuli Figurine. (Courtesy of the Ashmolean Museum)

and Porada admits that similar gestures are found on at least two ivory figurines from predynastic Egypt. Yet she does point out that the Hierakonpolis figurine shares two important features with figurines from Iran: the legs are truncated and lack feet and each figurine is carved from more than a single piece of stone. Based on these similarities, Porada suggests that the body of the figurine may have come

Fig. 19. Egyptian and Susan Serpent Motifs: A. Gebel Tarif, B. Susa, (After Capart 1905: fig. 33; Amiet 1972: fig. 488)

B

A

to Egypt via the Persian Gulf. She continues by maintaining that the head of the Hierakonpolis figurine is Egyptian in stylistic terms, but because there is a peg joining the head and body, the head could have been carved and attached long after the body was carved and imported.[45] It is therefore conceivable that the body was imported from Iran.

Because of the rarity of lapis lazuli; the positioning, shape, and size of the breasts, buttocks, and hands; the head and body being carved from separate pieces; and the absence of feet, the Hierakonpolis figurine may have been influenced more by the original shape of the material than any cultural influences. It is true that some motifs found in Egypt have their strongest parallels with contemporaneous motifs found in Susa (fig. 19), and that lapis lazuli probably passed through a Susan colony (Godin Tepe) in Iran before reaching Tepe Gawra (fig. 16),[46] which makes it possible that some features manifest in the Hierakonpolis figurine are attributable to Iranian influences. Even so, a review of lapis lazuli source locations (fig. 17), and recognition that Tepe Gawra had strong contacts with a number of sites in Iran,[47] indicate the most likely route connecting Egypt to Iran is via northern Mesopotamia, not through the Persian Gulf.

Lapis lazuli is also important because of its durability. Gold and silver are poor markers to discern trade routes because they are valuable metals that are usually melted down and reused. Silver and copper corrode in most environments and seldom survive in the archaeological record. In contrast, lapis lazuli was mainly carved into small beads and more rarely stamp seals; the statuette described above is very rare. Beads are too small to be reworked and are more likely to be overlooked when robbing a grave. If lapis lazuli was brought to a site in even relatively small amounts, then it is likely that these stones will survive in the archaeological record. The lack of lapis lazuli at so many sites suggests direct contact between sites or regions where lapis lazuli is plentiful.

It is clear that Egypt was procuring lapis lazuli, a rare and expensive commodity, but no one seems to know what the Egyptians were trading in return. We might begin by noting that the continued growth of Mesopotamian influence during the Naqada II period is matched by an increase in Upper Egyptian influence in Nubia. The importance of this influence during the Late Predynastic period and early in the First Dynasty is signified by the large-scale Nubian importation of copper tools, stone vessels, quartz maceheads with gold handles, cylinder seal impressions, wine jars, toilet vases,[48] and lapis lazuli all discovered in Nubian Group-A graves.[49] It seems that the graves of the Nubian rulers contained offerings nearly as rich as those found in the tombs of their counterparts in Egypt.[50] In turn, records from the Sixth Dynasty (ca. 2200 B.C.) show that Egypt imported incense, ivory, ebony, and leopard skins from Nubia.[51] Nubia was also known in dynastic times as a rich source of gold.[52] If Egypt was acquiring such items for trade with Mesopotamia, they would leave little if any trace today. The importance of Nubia as a source of exotic goods for trade is suggested by the fact that Group-A graves and Egyptian artifacts disappear from Nubia during the reign of Djer,[53] second king of the First Dynasty, when lapis lazuli disappears from Egypt.[54] Further, as previously mentioned in chapter 4, what is believed to be a piece of Nubian ware was uncovered at the Mesopotamian colony at Habuba Kabira in northern Syria. Other possible

Egyptian exports may have included textiles, beer, oils, and semiprecious stones, such as carnelian and turquoise.[55]

It should also be noted that lapis lazuli first appears at Tell Brak in association with the Grey Eye Temple. At Tell Brak there are four superimposed temples. The latest, dating to the Jamdat Nasr period, is known as the Eye Temple; the earliest dates to the Late Uruk period and is called the Red Eye Temple, which was succeeded by the Grey Eye Temple and then the White Eye Temple. The Grey Eye Temple, which dates to the end of the Late Uruk period or early in the Jamdat Nasr period,[56] was apparently the richest of the four, because it is honeycombed with tunnels presumably made by thieves in search of the rich temple offerings that had been deposited when the temple was filled during construction of a foundation for the White Eye Temple. As most of the artifacts recovered from the Grey Eye Temple had been smashed from the weight of this fill, Mallowan believed the thieves were interested primarily in gold[57]—gold that may have come from Egypt.

Egyptian prospectors most likely recovered their gold from erosional sediments located in the wadis of the Eastern Desert. The only gold that was actually mined during this time was probably done so as a byproduct of copper mining.[58] Even so, gold appears to have been plentiful in Egypt during the Late Predynastic period.[59] Indeed, the early dynastic name for Naqada itself was *Nbt*, which may be translated as "city of gold."[60] Outside of Egypt gold is rare at this time; eight small rings from a burial above Nahal Qana date to the fifth millennium,[61] one bead, in association with the previously mentioned silver bracelets, was discovered at Azor, and a few gold items have also been unearthed at Byblos from *énéolithique* burials (fig. 7).[62] The earliest gold artifacts from southern Mesopotamia are a piece of gold wire from Uruk dating to the Late Ubaid period. Gold continues to be rare as late as the end of the Late Uruk period with most of the surviving artifacts coming from Uruk.[63] In northern Mesopotamia, the earliest known gold is in the form of fluted beads from level XII at Tepe Gawra. As with lapis lazuli, gold is rare until Tepe Gawra X, at which time it is abundant. This level seems to correlate with Naqada IIa/b in Egypt, the only other place where lapis lazuli, faience, and gold are consistently found together so early in the Near East. No known sources of gold were worked in Mesopotamia, Syria, or Palestine at this time.[64] Sources of gold exist in Anatolia, Iran, and

Table 2: Aurian Silver Analyses, A. Tepe Gawra,
B. Abydos, & C. Provenance Unknown.

	Silver	Gold	Copper	Lead
A.	61.39%	38.05%	.56%	———
B.	60.40%	38.10%	1.50%	———
C.	61.35%	33.74%	4.90%	0.137%

Afghanistan, but there is little evidence that gold was being exploited in any quantities at these locations at such an early date.[65] If Mallowan was correct in his proposal that gold was plentiful in the Grey Eye Temple at Tell Brak, then the appearance of gold and lapis lazuli at this site would roughly coincide with an almost total disappearance of gold and lapis lazuli at Tepe Gawra VIII C, and with a continued abundance of both materials at the end of the Naqada III period and beginning of the First Dynasty in Egypt.

Some evidence may exist to suggest that Tepe Gawra X was importing at least some aurian silver from Egypt. According to Arthur Tobler, beads and a wolf's head made of electrum were found in graves dating to that level. Tobler had one of the beads analyzed. (See table 2, row A.)[66] When we compare results to those of the analyses of an early dynastic binding (row B),[67] and the rim casing of a vase dating to the Predynastic period (row C),[68] both from Egypt, the possibility arises that what Tobler describes as electrum is in reality either a natural-aurian silver or an artificially-alloyed silver from Egypt. Two of the three samples lack lead, which suggests they are a natural-aurian silver. Egypt is suggested as a source because it is the only place similar silver-to-gold ratios are commonly found in silver artifacts.

A review of pottery and raw materials seems to reveal an early trade route by land between Egypt and northern Mesopotamia via Palestine, but during the Naqada II period it appears that most trade between these two regions was by sea (fig. 16). The study of monkey-shaped figurines in the following section seems to support these conclusions.

MONKEYS AND MACEHEADS

Several hundred figurines representing lions, gazelles, ibex, bears, sheep, rams, bulls, cows, frogs, hares, foxes, hedgehogs, pigs, ducks, fish, dogs(?), asses, and monkeys were discovered in the Grey Eye Temple at Tell Brak in northern Mesopotamia.[1] The monkeys were of special importance, as only the lions and frogs were more common.[2] This is peculiar, because monkeys are not indigenous to Mesopotamia or the surrounding regions, and, except for a single monkey figurine found at Uruk, the Grey Eye Temple is the only place such figurines appear in Mesopotamia during the Late Uruk period (or early in the Jamdat Nasr period).[3] A few monkey figurines have been discovered at Susa, but these seem to be even later than those at Tell Brak.[4] Yet, as at Tell Brak, these figurines first appear just as lapis lazuli becomes abundant at each site.[5] Figurines and other kinds of monkey representations do become common in southern Mesopotamia, but not until the Early Dynastic period, when the animals may have been imported from India. The closest parallels for the monkey figurines recovered from the Grey Eye Temple come from Egypt and date to the beginning of the First Dynasty.[6] Monkey figurines are also important because they appear in northern Mesopotamia after the disappearance of the Mesopotamian colonies. The appearance of monkeys at Tell Brak, which is the only site with an abundance of lapis lazuli, at a time when lapis lazuli is still being acquired by Egypt suggests that direct contact continued between these two locations.

At Abydos, in Egypt, a bear-shaped figurine was discovered together with monkey figurines.[7] This, too, is peculiar because bears are not indigenous to Africa, and this is the only bear figurine known from Egypt before the Eighteenth Dynasty.[8] Although it is true, as

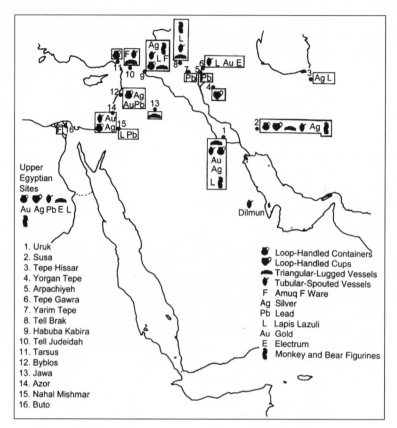

Fig. 20. Distribution of Figurines

M. E. L. Mallowan states, this figurine is not of Mesopotamian style;[9] the only place bear figurines are common is in the north: in the Grey Eye Temple at Tell Brak,[10] with one other coming from the Mesopotamian "colony" of Habuba Kabira.[11] Bear figurines are rare in southern Mesopotamia,[12] on the other hand, and neither monkey nor bear figurines are found around the Persian Gulf before dynastic times. Thus, the distribution of these figurines contributes to arguments for a northern connection between northern Mesopotamia and Egypt during predynastic times (fig. 20).

Maceheads may also be indicative of a link between northern Mesopotamia and Egypt. As discussed in chapter 3, the earliest pear-shaped maceheads seem to appear at Merimde in Lower Egypt at nearly the same time they appear in Palestine.[13] At approximately this same time, they make their first appearance in Iran and in level

XII at Tepe Gawra in northern Mesopotamia. They do not seem to make their way to Upper Egypt until the Naqada II period, nor in southern Mesopotamia until the Jamdat Nasr period, and they are absent from Persian Gulf sites.[14] Therefore, it is possible that the pear-shaped macehead reveals contacts between northern Mesopotamia and Egypt or Palestine or both.

W. A. Ward proposes that pear-shaped maceheads may have come originally from Anatolia or Iran and that the type may have evolved independently at different locations.[15] This seems unlikely because pear-shaped maceheads appear at about the same time at Tepe Gawra, Tepe Sialk, and Tell-i-Bakun (fig. 3),[16] a time when, as seals at Tepe Gawra indicate, trade was conducted among these three sites.[17] It is consequently more probable that this type of macehead spread through trade instead of developing more or less simultaneously at different locations.

Although the distribution patterns of pear-shaped maceheads and animal figurines are not in themselves definitive proof of trade routes, they support the idea of a northern Mesopotamia-Egypt route, especially because both items are absent from the Persian Gulf sites.

7

CYLINDER SEALS

The earliest cylinder seals found in Egypt are associated with Naqada IIc/d material.[1] Because of the striking similarities among them, there can be little doubt that Egyptian seals are either imports or copies of Mesopotamian and Iranian seals (figs. 21–23). The Egyptian seals were once thought to be most closely paralleled by Mesopotamian seals from the Jamdat Nasr period, but now, owing to more recent archaeological information, we know that many glyptic styles that had been assigned to the Jamdat Nasr period are also identified with the Late Uruk period.[2]

Contemporary seals or seal impressions have been found at Susa,[3] the Mesopotamian "colonies" in northern Syria,[4] Tell Judeidah,[5] Byblos, and Megiddo (figs. 3 and 7).[6] The seal impressions from Megiddo in northern Palestine might suggest that cylinder seals came to Egypt via Palestine. A comprehensive study of Palestinian seal impressions by Amnon Ben-Tor has led him to conclude that six impressions from Megiddo are contemporary with the seals from late predynastic Egypt.[7] Further, a comparison of Egyptian seals with Palestinian, Iranian, and Mesopotamian seals and seal impressions shows strong similarities among Egyptian, Mesopotamian, and Iranian seals, as well as an absence of similarities among Egyptian seals and Palestinian seal impressions (figs. 21–24).

In Ben-Tor's opinion the closest parallels for most of the Palestinian impressions come from Byblos, which, considering the proximity of the two areas, is understandable. He goes on to point out parallels between some motifs used on both the Biblite and Megiddo seals and those on seals from northern Mesopotamia and Iran, suggesting indirect contact.[8]

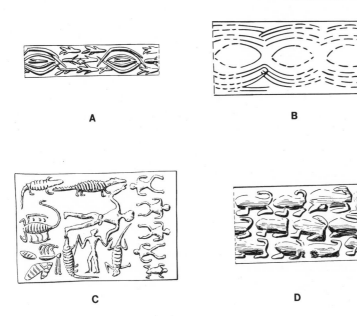

Fig. 21. Egyptian Seals: A. Unknown, B. Naqada, C–D. Unknown, E. Naga-ed-Der, F. Unknown, (After Kantor 1952: fig. 1D, 1A; Quibell 1905: pl. 59.14518; Kantor 1952: fig. 1E, 1B, 1F)

The use of cylinder seals should be considered. Palestinians impressed their seals on clay vessels before they were fired. Mesopotamians, on the other hand, generally impressed their seals on documents and jar sealings.[9] Egyptians appear to have worn their seals for adornment and, like the Mesopotamians, impressed their seals on clay to seal jars.[10]

From an analysis of predynastic Egyptian cylinder seals, Rainer M. Boehmer concludes that northern Mesopotamia and Iran are the most likely places of origin of the Egyptian seals.[11] He is supported by a later study of a stamp seal of apparent Naqada IIb date from Naga-ed-Der, tomb 7501. This seal's hemispheroid shape and motif suggest that it was imported from northern Mesopotamia or Iran.

A

B

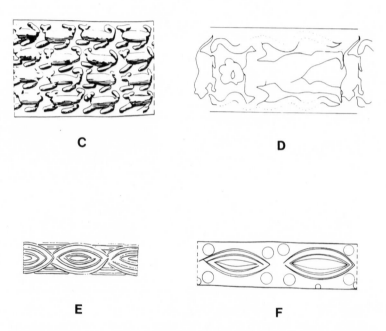

Fig. 22. Mesopotamian Seals: A. Nuzi, B. Khafaje, C. Telloh, D. Uruk, E. Fara, F. Habuba Kabira, (After Starr 1937: 41D; Kantor 1952: pl. 27H, 27J; Collon 1987: fig. 859; Martin 1988: fig. 82; Strommenger 1977: fig. 12)

C

D

E

F

Similar seals have been found at Tepe Gawra, Yorgan Tepe, Tepe Giyan, and Susa (figs. 3 and 25).[12] More support consists of a cylinder seal from Abusir el Meleq, grave 1035 (fig. 26A).[13] This seal bears a scene of a horned animal being pursued by hounds, a motif that is common on stamp seals from levels XI and X at Tepe Gawra (figs. 26B and C);[14] horned animals are also common on cylinder seals discovered at Jebel Aruda in northern Syria,[15] and a seal depicting two horned animals was discovered in Tomb U-j at Abydos.[16]

It would therefore appear doubtful that cylinder seals were transported to Egypt via Palestine. Instead, the evidence reviewed here

A

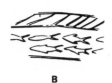

B

C

D

E

F

Fig. 23. Susan Seals: A–E. Susa, (After Boehmer 1974: fig. 19L; Ghirshman 1935: fig. 2; Amiet 1972: fig. 831, 595; Boehmer 1974: fig. 19N)

suggests that such seals reached Egypt via northern Syria and the sea. In addition, the distribution of hemispheroid stamp seals found between northern Mesopotamia and Susa is consistent with earlier evidence of trade between these two areas. The discovery of such a seal in Egypt and the absence of similar seals in Palestine also suggest seals were transported to Egypt via northern Syria and the sea (fig. 27).

Two seals found at sites in the Persian Gulf were originally dated to the Jamdat Nasr period. The first is a stamp seal recovered from a grave at Hajjar on the island of Bahrain. Based on a stylistic analysis,

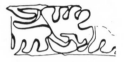

Fig. 24. Palestinian Seals: All seals from Megiddo (After Ben-Tor 1978: figs. 22, 38, 29, 41, 42, 47, 71)

the seal is of Jamdat Nasr type, but artifacts in the grave date from the Kassite period (ca. 1500 B.C.). It is now thought that the seal was already old when it was brought to Bahrain, after which it may have been recut. The second seal is similar to seals of the Piedmont Jamdat Nasr style, but as it is made of frit, it has been compared to an Elamite glyptic from the late second millennium B.C.[17] Mesopotamian seals are absent from Persian Gulf sites, therefore, before the end of the Jamdat Nasr period.

Finally, foreign motifs most commonly found in Egypt are representative of northern Mesopotamia and Susa, and when we compare this trend with the distributions of artifacts already discussed in this study, we notice a recurring pattern that does seem to connect Egypt with Mesopotamia via northern Syria. A brief study of architectural features will reinforce this pattern.

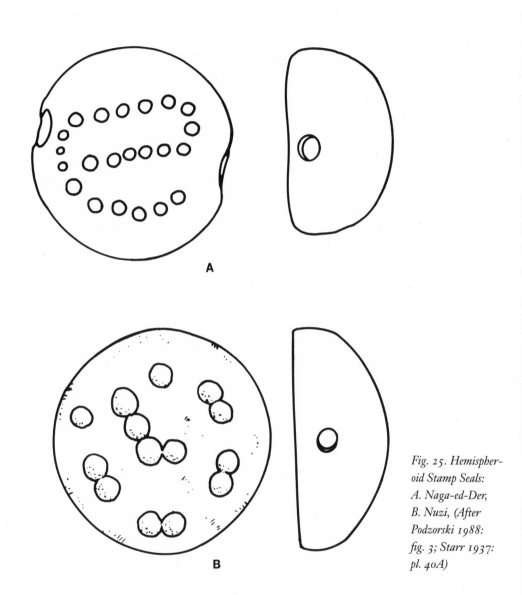

Fig. 25. Hemispheroid Stamp Seals: A. Naga-ed-Der, B. Nuzi, (After Podzorski 1988: fig. 3; Starr 1937: pl. 40A)

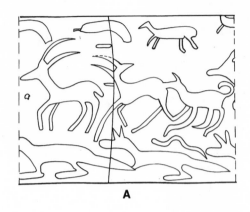

A

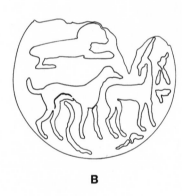

B

C

Fig. 26. Seals Bear-
ing Horned Ani-
mals: A. Abusir el
Meleq, B–C. Tepe
Gawra, (After
Boehmer 1974: fig.
9; Tobler 1950: pls.
168.156, 169.163)

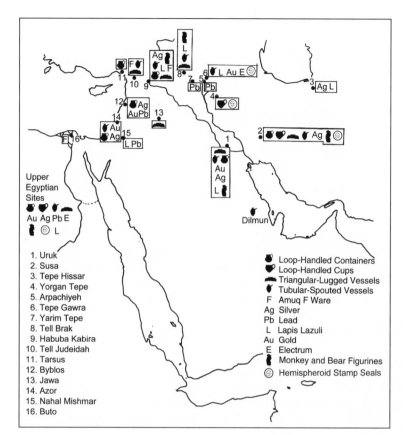

Upper Egyptian Sites

Au Ag Pb E
L

1. Uruk
2. Susa
3. Tepe Hissar
4. Yorgan Tepe
5. Arpachiyeh
6. Tepe Gawra
7. Yarim Tepe
8. Tell Brak
9. Habuba Kabira
10. Tell Judeidah
11. Tarsus
12. Byblos
13. Jawa
14. Azor
15. Nahal Mishmar
16. Buto

🝔 Loop-Handled Containers
🝕 Loop-Handled Cups
🝖 Triangular-Lugged Vessels
🝗 Tubular-Spouted Vessels
F   Amuq F Ware
Ag Silver
Pb Lead
L   Lapis Lazuli
Au Gold
E   Electrum
🝘 Monkey and Bear Figurines
◎ Hemispheroid Stamp Seals

Fig. 27. Distribution of Hemispheroid Seals

ARCHITECTURE

Henri Frankfort was the first to point out the similarities between the temples of Mesopotamia and the large First Dynasty tombs with crenelated facades in Egypt (figs. 28, 29);[1] these similarities go beyond the elaborate recessed panelling of the outer walls. The custom of building intricate facades with small bricks, as seen on at least one Egyptian tomb, is characteristic of Mesopotamian architecture throughout the Uruk and Jamdat Nasr periods. The use of three rows of stretchers alternating as a rule with one row of headers on the face of the facade, the manner in which a plinth or platform at the base of a structure is built, and the use of short timbers inserted horizontally to strengthen the niches are all features shared by Mesopotamian temples and some Egyptian tombs. The closest parallels for all of the features recorded from these First Dynasty tombs are from Mesopotamian temples built during the Jamdat Nasr period.[2]

The earliest example of this style of construction in Egypt is the early dynastic tomb of Neith-hotep at Naqada (ca. 3050 B.C.). This tomb is composed of a burial chamber with four subsidiary rooms surrounded by sixteen magazines (fig. 29). The five central rooms of Neith-hotep's tomb are not an integral part of the crenelated facade. The magazine cross-walls interbond with the crenelated wall but not with the walls of the five central rooms.[3] The entrance to the central section of this tomb is bricked up, and one of the cross-walls abuts against this section of wall suggesting that the central chamber was completed, filled, and sealed before the crossing walls and crenelated exterior were built. The cross-wall, however, only covers about half of the original entrance. Therefore, its purpose was not to conceal the entrance to the burial chamber. There does not appear to be any

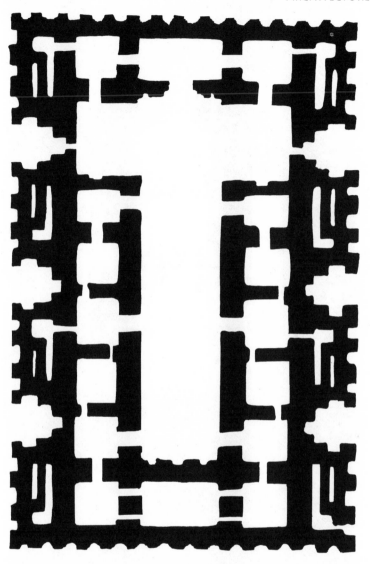

Fig. 28. Mesopota-mian Temple from Uruk. (After Amiet 1980: fig. 978)

precedent for this type of a two-stage construction technique, nor is any structural advantage gained by building cross-walls in this fash-ion. A tomb, such as Neith-hotep's, that is built above ground and has a rather simple plan could have been constructed more quickly and efficiently as an integrated unit. This tomb is also unusual in that the sixteen magazines were left empty; only the five central rooms contained burial equipment.[4]

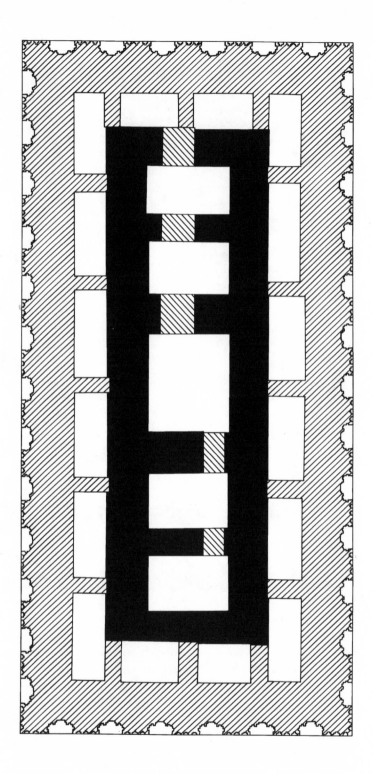

Fig. 29. Neith-hotep's Tomb, ca. 3100 B.C. (After Borchardt 1898: pl. 14/15)

Neith-hotep's tomb also contains a number of other unusual features. For example, five different sizes of bricks were used in its construction. In contrast, most other Egyptian tombs were built with only one size of brick.[5] As previously mentioned, the bricks were laid in three layers of stretchers alternating with one of headers in some sections of the tomb; this feature is rare in other tombs.[6] In addition, it has never been explained how the plinth evolved in Egyptian architecture, whereas its evolution is obvious in Mesopotamian architecture. In regard to the central section or core, the walls are twice as thick as the magazine walls, nearly as thick as the exterior crenelated wall, and appear to be much larger than the interior walls of any other predynastic or First Dynasty tomb (compare figs. 29 and 30). The walls of this chamber are large enough to constitute the outer walls of a separate tomb. It appears as if this structure embodies two different building traditions. If we remove this central section, the structure is similar to a classical Mesopotamian temple with a large central cell surrounded by smaller rooms (compare figs. 28 and 31). In contrast, the central section is similar to the royal tombs at Abydos of the Predynastic period. It is as if an Egyptian burial chamber was built above ground and then surrounded by a Mesopotamian temple.[7]

It has been argued that Egyptian reed or wooden buildings were the prototype for these later crenelated facades. The recessed sections of a crenelated facade are believed to represent wooden or reed walls while the projecting members represent the bracing for the structure. This style is supposed to have been adapted to brick buildings at some unknown period, becoming more intricate with the passage of time until finally culminating with the crenelated facades of First Dynasty tombs.[8] The difficulty with this theory is a dearth of evidence to support it. W. M. F. Petrie believes that he had discovered fragmentary remains of such a "panelled house," which had been dismantled and reused for coffins and roofing in tombs dating to the First Dynasty. He proposes that these boards are a prototype of a palace facade structure.[9] Frankfort responds by pointing out that the shapes of the planks and type of fastenings used to join them suggest that they are salvaged remains of one or more Nile river vessels. A more recent study of these planks by Steve Vinson supports Frankfort's interpretation.[10]

Other evidence that appears to portray the exterior facade of a crenelated or panelled palace includes representations on seals, ste-

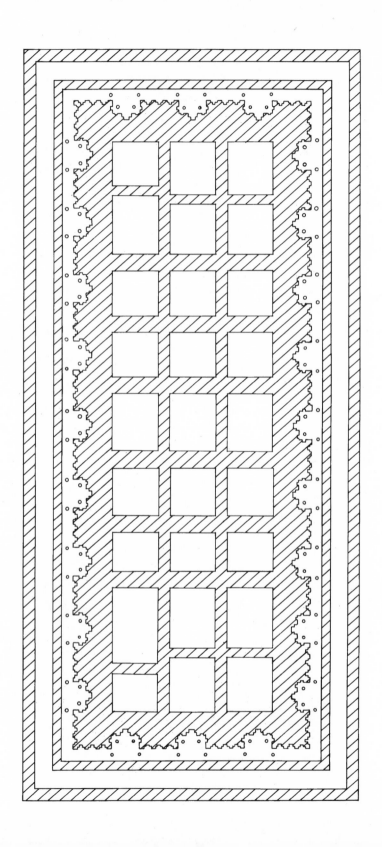

Fig. 30. First Dynasty Tomb of Hor Aha at Saqqara, Tomb 3357, ca. 3050 B.C. (After Emery 1939: pl. 1)

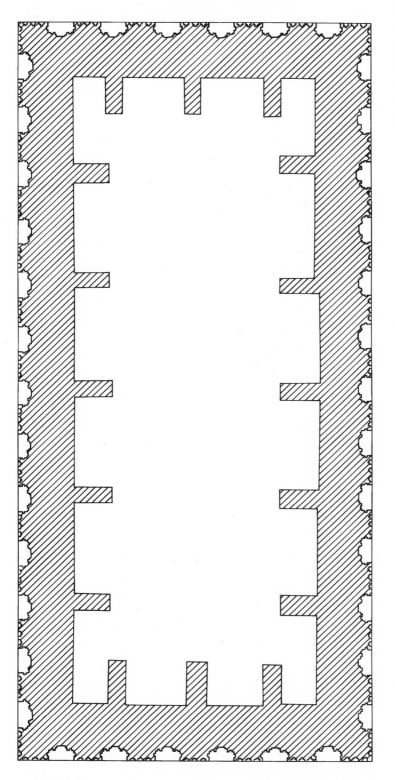

Fig. 31. Neith-hotep's Tomb with the Core Removed. (Detail after Borchardt 1898: pl. 14/15)

lae, and sarcophagi with the earliest representations appearing on *ser-ekhs*. In Egyptian iconography, the *serekh* encloses the Horus name of the king. The lowest element of the *serekh* is considered to be the palace facade, which represents a tomb or palace of the king.[11] This interpretation contains a number of flaws. The earliest *serekhs* appear during the Naqada III period, but these representations are so rudimentary in design and execution that it is impossible to know what object inspired their creation.[12] The *serekh* and other "palace-facade" representations that date to the First Dynasty, however, are more detailed, but because these depictions are only two-dimensional renderings, they reveal little of the actual appearance of such a building and only depict an entrance area, not all of the exterior.[13]

These First Dynasty motifs are also usually associated with Lower Egypt, especially at Giza (fig. 6).[14] The closest contemporary parallel to the Egyptian palace-facade is engraved on a cylinder seal from Tell Billa in northern Mesopotamia. The similarity shared by these motifs is not limited to the recessed facade but also extends to their floral decorations.[15] The main difficulty with associating the earliest motifs with a crenelated structure is that we lack detailed representations of the palace-facade motif before the First Dynasty. So, the sudden appearance of these detailed motifs in Egypt is roughly contemporary with the earliest construction of a tomb with a crenelated facade. As with the crenelated tombs, too little time would have passed to allow a simple prototype to evolve into the intricate-crenelated facade seen on First Dynasty tombs. We are then faced with the question of whether or not this later palace-facade motif is of Egyptian origin, a Mesopotamian import, or an Egyptian motif adapted owing to Mesopotamian influence.

One secular building with a crenelated facade that dates to the Early Dynastic period has been discovered in Egypt. This structure was uncovered within the townsite at Hierakonpolis. The size and intricacies of this facade are similar to those of Neith-hotep's tomb and Tomb 3357 at Saqqara, and, because niching becomes simpler with the passage of time in Egypt, this structure is believed to be roughly contemporary with these two tombs. Seal impressions recovered within the gateway and above the floor date to the late Second or early Third Dynasty. Therefore, the structure cannot be any later than this period.[16] We are then faced with the previously mentioned problem that this gateway, the tombs, the palace-facade motif, and Petrie's boards all date to the First Dynasty. All of the available evidence suggests that this type of structure suddenly appeared in Egypt at the beginning of the First Dynasty.

This evidence bolsters Frankfort's argument that nothing from predynastic architecture would have evolved into such crenelated structures by the time of the First Dynasty.[17] We may also add that the earliest evidence for brick structures in Egypt comes from the town of Naqada and dates to the end of the Naqada I period; according to Petrie, the builders were careless about the squareness and angles of their buildings.[18] Decorative palettes from the Naqada III period contain representations of walled enclosures that must also have been made of brick; like the buildings at Naqada, they too have irregular shapes (fig. 32). It is also true that brick tombs, such as Tomb U-j at Abydos, were being built by the end of the Naqada IIIa period, but these structures are still rather crude in their shape and construction techniques as compared to the tombs with niched facades.[19] Finally, these representations and structures lack any resemblance to the later crenelated buildings in shape or quality of construction, which argues against the possibility that such an evolution took place in Upper Egypt.

In Mesopotamia, however, the development of crenelated architecture can be followed in detail from simple, widely spaced recesses that date as early as the Ubaid period to elaborate recessing in the Uruk and Jamdat Nasr periods, a process taking about a millennia.[20] In contrast to this orderly and consistent evolution in Mesopotamia, the earliest crenelated architecture in Egypt is the most complex, and it is simplified rather quickly,[21] suggesting that this architectural style moved to Egypt from Mesopotamia. If such an evolution did take place in Egypt in the 150 years between the construction of Tomb U-j and Neith-hotep's tomb, then the Egyptians perfected in 150 years what it took the Mesopotamians a millennia to perfect and without leaving evidence for such an evolution.

Because Neith-hotep's tomb and Mesopotamian-type artifacts and motifs are found at Naqada, only a few kilometers south of the Wadi Hammamat, Frankfort further proposed that the most likely route connecting Egypt with Mesopotamia was the sea route around Arabia, and then via the Wadi.[22] Under scrutiny this does not appear likely.

In fact, a number of factors support the possibility that the earliest tomb with a niched facade in Egypt was a product of the Delta. Walter Emery believed that Neith-hotep was a princess of Lower

Fig. 32. Depiction of an Egyptian Fortress. (Detail after Emery 1961: fig. 74, and Petrie 1953: pl. G)

Egypt and that Narmer married her to legitimize his rule of that region.[23] Even if Emery is incorrect, Neith-hotep's name comes from that of the goddess Neith of Sais,[24] a town in the western Delta (fig. 7), which seems to indicate some connection between this queen and the Delta. Thus it would be understandable if she were buried in a tomb similar to those used in the Delta. The internal structure of Neith-hotep's tomb also raises doubts that her tomb was adapted directly from a Mesopotamian building for use in Upper Egypt. As previously mentioned, predynastic graves of Upper Egypt usually consist of a shallow oval or circular hole with some matting or wooden reinforcement. During the Naqada II period, these pits were enlarged and eventually lined with bricks, and by the Naqada III period, at the royal cemetery of Abydos, these brick-lined pits had evolved into great underground chambers covered by low flat-topped mounds of sand and surrounded by a flat brick wall. Therefore, even though there is some similarity between Neith-hotep's tomb and contemporary tombs at Abydos, we must ask why the burial chamber of Neith-hotep's tomb was located aboveground, especially when all later tombs with niched facades have subterranean burial chambers.[25] One possible reason is that her type of tomb was customarily used in an area with a high water table, where it would be impossible to build a subterranean chamber. The most likely such place would be the Egyptian Delta.

The sudden appearance of Egyptian tombs with crenelated facades is one of the strongest arguments for this style of architecture having its origins in Mesopotamia. On the other hand, contrary to earlier arguments using this as evidence for southern Egyptian contacts with Mesopotamia, it is also one of the strongest arguments supporting the Delta as the area where niched-facade architecture first arrived from Mesopotamia. In an evaluation of Neith-hotep's tomb, Frankfort writes that Egyptians were "familiar with every refinement of which the material was capable."[26] Emery, when comparing the workmanship of crenelated facades of Egyptian tombs to that of Mesopotamian temples, states that "Egypt's superiority is beyond question." Emery continues by pointing out that the brick sizes used in Egypt and Mesopotamia are different proportions and that such an evolution took place in a location between Upper Egypt and Mesopotamia.[27] If this is all true, the construction of a structure as large as Neith-hotep's tomb (53.4 by 26.7 meters) with the quality of workmanship inherent in the intricate brickwork of the facade would have taken an experienced workforce. As no antecedents exist for the previously mentioned construction techniques in Upper Egypt, the only place from which such experience could have been gained would have been the Delta. The Delta's location between the Mesopotamian colonies in northern Syria and Upper Egypt would have also provided an intermediate location necessary for the evolution that was referred to by Emery.

Although, as previously mentioned, niched tombs appeared suddenly in Upper Egypt at the beginning of the First Dynasty, by this time most artifacts and motifs inspired by Mesopotamia had either disappeared or been assimilated by the indigenous culture.[28] Mesopotamian pottery, cylinder seals, and lapis lazuli are all small, easily movable items that could have been obtained early on through trade or as spoils of war during the Naqada II and III periods, whereas the knowledge to build such large and elaborate tombs, along with an experienced workforce to build them, more likely would have been acquired as the result of a dramatic sociopolitical event, such as the fall of the western Deltaic towns. This would explain why niched tombs suddenly appear so much later than do the other Mesopotamian materials. Furthermore, lapis lazuli continued to be imported through the beginning of the First Dynasty, and the appearance of these tombs also seems to coincide roughly with the appearance of monkey figurines in the Grey Eye Temple at Tell Brak. Thus, crenelated tombs may be a further indication of continued contact between Egypt and Mesopotamia during early dynastic times.

Other archaeological evidence supports the possibility that Mesopotamian architecture in Egypt first appeared in the Delta. Clay cones and pegs were commonly used during the Uruk period to decorate niches, walls, and columns of Mesopotamian temples. At the deltaic site of Buto, fragments of such cones and pegs have been recovered. According to Thomas von der Way, the excavator, the cones have their closest parallels with cones found at Susa. Clay bottles were also recovered from the site, and may have been used as both a type of structural support and, like the cones, for decoration. These bottles are associated with temple construction in southern Mesopotamia and Susa.[29] Crenelated architecture, clay cones, and clay pegs have also been found at Habuba Kabira/Tell Qannas in northern Syria.[30]

Finally, we may have some of the earliest evidence for a building constructed with arches at Nineveh. This building was dated to the Late Uruk period based on the large number of beveled-rim bowls found on the site.[31] Ann L. Perkins redated it to the Early Dynastic II period primarily on the basis of an absence of parallels for this type of structure during the Late Uruk period,[32] but in a more recent study Guillermo Algaze agrees with the dating submitted by the original excavators.[33] Arches have also been discovered in a building of the same period at Tell Qannas in northern Syria.[34]

Petrie, in his final report on the site, describes tomb T 15 at Naqada by stating that "in the pit a vaulted brick chamber has been built,"[35] and in one of Petrie's notebooks next to a sketch of tomb T 23 is written "brick arch in."[36] Both tombs date to the Naqada II period. Barry Kemp has reservations concerning the use of arches in these two tombs. In regard to T 15, he points out that Petrie fails to mention a vaulted brick chamber in his notebooks. In regard to T 23, if the arch refers to the doorway, if the thickness of the walls

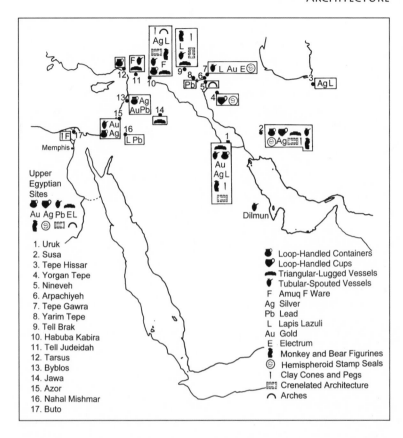

1. Uruk
2. Susa
3. Tepe Hissar
4. Yorgan Tepe
5. Nineveh
6. Arpachiyeh
7. Tepe Gawra
8. Yarim Tepe
9. Tell Brak
10. Habuba Kabira
11. Tell Judeidah
12. Tarsus
13. Byblos
14. Jawa
15. Azor
16. Nahal Mishmar
17. Buto

Loop-Handled Containers
Loop-Handled Cups
Triangular-Lugged Vessels
Tubular-Spouted Vessels
F   Amuq F Ware
Ag   Silver
Pb   Lead
L   Lapis Lazuli
Au   Gold
E   Electrum
Monkey and Bear Figurines
Hemispheroid Stamp Seals
Clay Cones and Pegs
Crenelated Architecture
Arches

Fig. 33. Distribution of Architectural Features

are constant throughout the tomb, if the tomb had a depth equal to tomb T 15, and if all of Petrie's measurements are correct, Kemp points out that the arch will have a width of only 60 centimeters. In his opinion, "such a small, rough arch need not conjure up anything as spectacular as a vaulted chamber."[37] Although Kemp's argument is well considered and logical, it is based primarily upon a number of assumptions. Thus, considering that both tombs purported to have arches date to a period when Mesopotamian influences appear in Upper and Lower Egypt, and when arches were used in a Mesopotamian building in northern Syria and at Nineveh, it is possible that Petrie's original observations were correct about the possibility of arches being used in these two Egyptian tombs. If Kemp is correct, on the other hand, and tomb T 15 included just a small, rough arch over the doorway, such an arch still could have been an unsuccessful attempt to emulate an architectural feature being used in the Delta.

None of the architectural elements discussed above have been found in the Persian Gulf region. The earliest known architectural features from Mesopotamia that have been discovered there date much later, to the Early Dynastic period.[38] Thus, such features, like the artifacts previously discussed, support a trade route that extended from northern Mesopotamia to Egypt (fig. 33). A review of boat motifs should reinforce this pattern.

BOAT MOTIFS

Various motifs that are attributed to Mesopotamia appear in Egypt during the Naqada II and III periods.[1] Most of these representations were probably brought to Egypt as engravings on cylinder seals and, as pointed out in chapter 6, came to Egypt via northern Mesopotamia. In contrast to the motifs previously mentioned, motifs representing high-ended ships have been used to support the argument that Sumerians sailed around Arabia to make contact with predynastic Egypt. The high-ended ships on the handle of the Gebel el Arak knife, the mural in Tomb 100 at Hierakonpolis, and rock drawings near the Wadi Hammamat are the most commonly cited examples of "foreign ships" in predynastic Egypt. The close proximity of these three groups of representations to the Wadi Hammamat is one of the primary reasons it has been argued to be the path through which the Sumerians entered Egypt.

The war scene on one side of the Gebel el Arak knife handle is divided into four registers. The two upper registers depict men with shaved heads or short hair fighting men with long hair (fig. 34). Two high-ended vessels appear in the third register, and in the fourth are three sickle-shaped vessels similar to those commonly found on Naqada II pottery. The bodies of four men appear between the third and fourth registers. The first interpretation of this war scene was presented by Georges Bénédite. He writes that representations at Susa and Telloh provide the closest parallels for the men with shaved heads. He also points out the strong similarities between the two high-ended vessels in the third register with representations of vessels on Mesopotamian cylinder seals (fig. 35). Bénédite includes a detailed description of the "foreign boats," stating that the bow is to

Fig. 34. Gebel el Arak Handle, Reverse Side. (After Yadin 1965: 116)

the left and the stern to the right. Secured to the bow by three ties is an inclined mast surmounted by a disk halved by a vertical bar; this disk represents the pulley through which the main halyard passes. To the right of the mast is a vaulted cabin adjacent to a pole bearing an ensign. Near the stern is a short stanchion surmounted by a crescent that functions as a stand for a steering oar or quarter rudder. Finally, the sternpost is crowned by an old totem ensign (fig. 36).[2] Bénédite's interpretation of the motifs on the Gebel el Arak knife, and the fact that this knife was found in Upper Egypt, have been used to argue for a southern trade route between southern Egypt and Sumer.[3]

Fig. 35. Mesopotamian River Boat. (After Hermann 1968: fig. 5a)

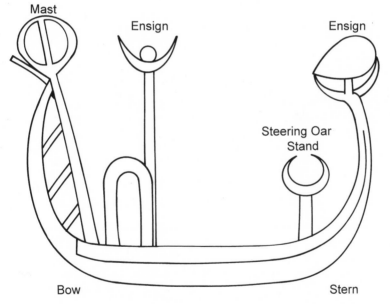

Fig. 36. Bénédite's Interpretation of a High-Ended Boat. (After Bénédite 1916: fig. 10)

On the other hand, recent studies have pointed out errors in Bénédite's interpretation and provide new interpretations. William Smith suggests that the warriors with long hair or side locks depict Libyans, and that the warriors with short hair are from southern Egypt. He believes it is possible that the Gebel el Arak knife records a local struggle between these two groups.[4] Unfortunately, we have little definitive evidence concerning hair styles and how they changed from region to region during the Predynastic period. Identifications based on hair style, therefore, are, at best, unreliable.

In regard to vessels, Bruce Williams and Thomas Logan contend that Bénédite reversed the bow and stern of the two vessels in the third register, and cite as a parallel a boat relief on the handle of a knife in the Metropolitan Museum of Art that displays the same arrangement of a pole attached by three ties to one extremity of a vessel (fig. 37). On this relief we see a man sitting with his back to this pole—and he is grasping a steering oar. As the steering oar is always

Fig. 37. Metropolitan Museum Knife Handle. (After Williams and Logan 1987: fig. 1)

located in the stern of a boat, the end of the boat on the Gebel el Arak knife at which Bénédite locates the "mast" should therefore be the stern.[5]

There has been in any case strong opposition to Bénédite's interpretation of the "tied pole," here surmounted by a disk, as a mast. Vandier asserts that no such apparatus existed during this time in Egyptian history.[6] According to Williams and Logan, the pole was affixed to the stern to add rigidity and to stabilize the vessel.[7] If this is true, then such poles should be common on vessels of this period, and we should also see them change as the vessels to which they are attached evolve over time. The only known Egyptian representations of this "stabilizing pole" on high-ended vessels come from the Gebel el Arak and Metropolitan Museum knife handles; representations on Mesopotamian cylinder seals, however, do reveal changes in the way poles are depicted. The boat in figure 38 has a flat bottom with two upcurving ends. A pole is attached to each curved end by what may be accepted as two ties. In this case, the poles probably helped to strengthen and stabilize the vessel as Williams and Logan suggest. This would be true especially if the vessel was made of reed bundles lashed together. Reeds are buoyant and pliant, but, unlike wood, they have little rigidity. Therefore, pulling both ends of the vessel inward to form crescents and then tying them to a pole to hold them fast would have increased tension throughout the boat and further tightened the lashings around the reed bundles. This would have resulted in a stronger and more stable craft. Perhaps from an inherent human desire to decorate utilitarian objects, an emblem was mounted on the

Fig. 38. Mesopotamian Boat with Two Stabilizing Poles. (After Qualls 1981: fig. 230)

stern pole. As time passed and reed was replaced by wood, or a more effective way of constructing reed vessels evolved, the need for stabilizing poles presumably would have disappeared. By this time, however, the pole surmounted by an emblem may have evolved into a purely decorative motif, or had acquired a new utilitarian purpose as a religious, political, or geographic standard. The only other explanation for such a pole in the stern would be that as the need for this means of stabilization passed, the stern became a storage area for a mast. But this is improbable, because all of the Mesopotamian representations of boats with stabilizing poles that I have studied depict men paddling, poling, or punting; none depicts a boat under sail. Moreover, the emblem does not always sit directly on top of the pole but is sometimes attached to the curved end of the stern (fig. 35), making its identification as a decorative motif or an insignia even more likely.

The prow of each high-ended vessel on the Gebel el Arak handle is surmounted by an insignia (fig. 34). Its closest parallel is the early dynastic hieroglyph of Letopolis (⊖̣),[8] which is located near the apex of the Delta. It is also important to note that Bénédite interprets the crescent on the short stanchion of the Gebel el Arak vessel as a support for a steering oar, but Frederick van Doorninck has pointed out that the crescent sits atop a disk-shaped object, not a stanchion; it is perhaps a bull's head (figs. 34, 39).[9] This observation is supported by a comparison of the "horns" of this "bull's head" with the skull on the end of the middle vessel in the fourth register (fig. 34). The crescent and the skull's horns are similar in size, shape, and orientation. The bull was a symbol of royalty during the Late Predynastic period. These heads, therefore, may indicate two groups of royal ships representing opposing kingdoms.

If the low-mounted crescents on both high-ended vessels are the remains of skulls or are carved figureheads of bulls, as on the prows of the sickle-shaped boats, it would mean that, except for these symbols of royalty depicted on both types of vessels, the high-ended boats display three different insignias and the sickle-shaped boats have none. Insignias are commonly displayed on sickle-shaped boats on Naqada II pottery.[10] According to Petrie, they are either port signs or religious emblems;[11] so, it seems reasonable that they were to perform the same function on the knife handle. The size of these insignias, and the placement of the high-ended ships on the handle, would make it easy for any of the peoples of the high-ended ships to recog-

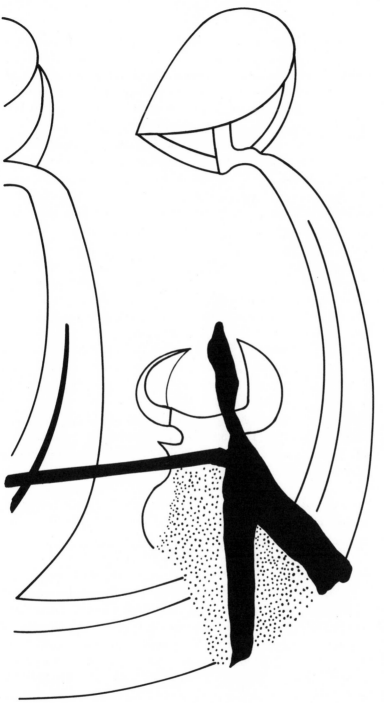

Fig. 39. Bull's Skull? (Detail after Yadin 1965: 116; see also Gardner 1961, pl. 20.)

nize which of their towns or villages had fought the Upper Egyptians. In contrast, the sickle-shaped vessels are relegated to the bottom register. Specific insignias for sickle-shaped vessels would not have any symbolic meaning to the Lower Egyptians and would be unnecessary; the shape of the vessel alone would identify the enemy to the casual observer. It has been proposed that this knife handle and other similar artifacts were carved by Elamite craftsmen in Upper Egypt.[12] Such an explanation would explain the Mesopotamian motifs seen on this knife handle, but it seems unlikely that if an Elamite craftsman was carving for an Upper Egyptian king he would omit the ensigns commonly seen on representations of such vessels nor would he place the Upper Egyptian ships in an inferior position in the bottom register.

As previously mentioned, the fact that this knife was discovered in Upper Egypt has been used to argue for a southern trade route. Unfortunately, this knife was not found *in situ*. It was purchased from a dealer in Cairo, who claims it was discovered in the vicinity of Gebel el Arak.[13] Therefore, a large part of the evidence for a southern trade route is based on a statement given by an antiquities dealer. In fact, we do not know for certain where this knife handle was originally discovered. For all we know the dealer gave a false location to protect his source of illicit antiquities. These carved handles are rare; the provenance for most is in doubt, and most are engraved with motifs that have strong similarities to Mesopotamian motifs. We must then ask ourselves if it is not possible that these handles were carved by craftsmen in the Delta and brought to Upper Egypt as spoils of war.

If we accept the possibility that the Gebel el Arak handle was carved by a craftsman from the Delta, it would explain the strong similarity between the insignia on the prow of the high-ended ships and the hieroglyph of Letopolis; it would explain the carver's familiarity with the insignias displayed on the high-ended vessels and the lack of insignias displayed on the sickle-shaped vessels; and it would explain the strong Mesopotamian influence that is evident in the design of the high-ended vessels and the strong similarities between the master of animals depicted on the opposite side of the handle and a motif commonly found on Mesopotamian cylinder seals (see respectively, figs. 40A and C). The sudden appearance and disappearance of such distinctive vessels in Egypt, at a time when similar vessels were common in Mesopotamia, by itself lends support to the possi-

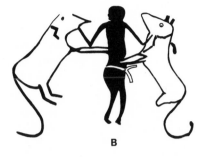

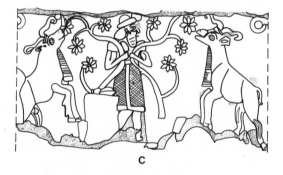

bility of Mesopotamian influence. If we add to this the possibility that Buto in the Nile Delta served as an important Egyptian importer of Mesopotamian goods,[14] and at the same time adopted various Mesopotamian architectural features,[15] it would be understandable that its people would also have learned some Mesopotamian ship construction techniques and copied the motifs used to decorate watercraft. In fact, the vague similarities between the knife handle and the Hierakonpolis painting is the only apparent connection between the Gebel el Arak knife and southern Egypt.

The Hierakonpolis mural was painted on wall A of what is now believed to be a tomb of the Naqada IId period (fig. 41).[16] The primary difficulty with evaluating this painting is coping with the large number of conflicting interpretations. According to V. Gordon Childe, the wall painting depicts the same naval battle, involving the same types of boats, that appears on the Gebel el Arak knife. Petrie interprets it as a depiction of the same peoples but a different battle. He believes the mural portrays a victory of the Upper Egyptians, the

Fig. 40. Master of Animals Motifs: A. Gebel el Arak handle, B. Hierakonpolis Mural, C. Near Uruk, (After Emery 1961: fig. 1 and author's photographs; detail from Quibell and Green 1902: pl. 75; after Collon 1987: fig. 6)

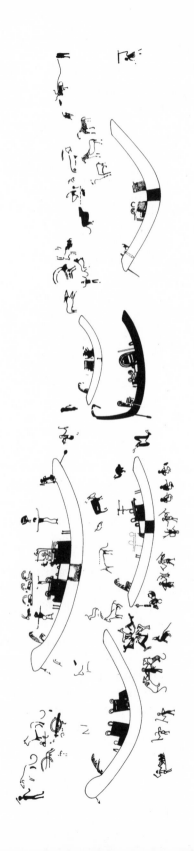

Fig. 41. Hierakon-
polis Mural. (After
Quibell and Green
1902 pls. 75–78)

red men in the sickle-shaped boats, over the invaders, symbolized by the black man in the black boat. Although the black boat has only one high end, Petrie maintains that it is the same type of high-ended craft found on the Gebel el Arak handle. Unlike Childe and Petrie, Henri Frankfort appears to have reservations about the Hierakonpolis mural. He proposes that the high-ended boat type on the Gebel el Arak knife is the same craft on which foreigners traveled up the Red Sea to Egypt. He agrees that the black boat on the mural is foreign, but only because a boat with such a high stern and low prow is otherwise unknown. I have found no other references by Frankfort to the Hierakonpolis mural. In a later publication, he states that the battle scene on the Gebel el Arak knife is without parallel in predynastic times. Helene Kantor submits that similar motifs on the Gebel el Arak knife and the Hierakonpolis mural are derived from a common fund of late Gerzean subjects,[17] and also states that the black boat has a high stern and low prow and is a well-known example of a Mesopotamian boat.

In fact, the only motifs on the mural that have possible Mesopotamian parallels are the black boat and the master of animals. The master of animals on the mural bears only a superficial resemblance to the one on the Gebel el Arak knife (see respectively, figs. 40B and A). He no longer wears the headdress, beard, or robe, but a simple codpiece. It is clear that this motif has been completely assimilated by the Naqada II culture.[18] The continued insistence that the black boat is of the same type as or even similar to Mesopotamian craft has never been substantiated. As for the black boat, no evidence exists that Mesopotamians of the Late Uruk period ever used a boat that has one extremity so much higher than the other. Furthermore, it becomes difficult to accept the view that the black boat is of a foreign type when no agreement can be reached as to which end is the bow and which is the stern.

But, if we remove the raised end from the black boat and then compare it to one of the Egyptian sickle-shaped boats on the mural, we see a number of similarities (fig. 42). Each boat has a crescent-shaped hull; each boat is equipped with a mooring line, a fender, or some type of decoration hanging from the bow; and at the bow of each boat a branch shades each cabin. Other similarities include the location of the cabins amidships, the shape of one of the cabins on the black boat and those on the other boats, and an awning between the cabins. Finally, on the sickle-shaped vessel two vertical parallel

Fig. 42. Sickle-Shaped and High-Prowed Boats from the Hierakonpolis Mural. (Detail from Quibell and Green 1902: pl. 75)

lines are placed on either side of the cabins while on the black boat two vertical parallel lines are placed on the high-ended side of the cabins and a horseshoe-shaped object is placed toward the other end.

From the foregoing it seems clear that the only differences between the black vessel and the sickle-shaped vessel are their colors, the rounded cabins, and the high end of the black vessel. We even have at least one good example of an Egyptian craft with a high and low end on a piece of Naqada I pottery (fig. 43), and rounded cabins are not uncommon in Egyptian iconography.[19] More importantly, it is possible to explain the use of the black boat motif in the context of Egyptian culture. William Smith interprets the mural as a funeral scene, and Williams and Logan interpret it as the Heb-Sed ceremony with the bark procession as its core.[20] In such a context, it is plausible that the ceremonial bark would be altered so as to be readily distinguished. At the very least, we can say that no solid evidence exists to support the theory that the Hierakonpolis mural records a conflict between Egyptians and foreigners, nor that the black vessel has any direct links with Mesopotamian craft of the Late Uruk period.

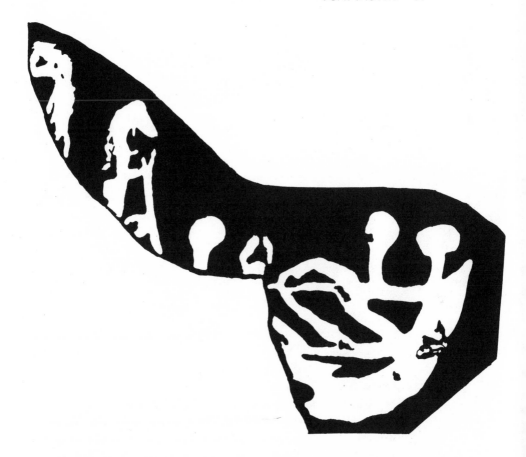

The theory that Mesopotamians made their way to Egypt via the Wadi Hammamat has, to a large extent, been based upon Hans Winkler's study of the rock drawings along the Wadi. Winkler's evidence for the arrival of what he terms "Eastern Invaders" can be summarized in one sentence: "They are connected with a form of boat, the square-boat, foreign to Egypt, well known in early Mesopotamia." Of all the representations Winkler published, one in particular was "strikingly similar" to the high-ended boats of the Gebel el Arak knife and the representation of a boat on a Mesopotamian cylinder seal (figs. 34, 35, 44).[21] Winkler's single criterion for identifying a foreign craft is that "the hull is straight; prow and stern are bent upwards in a rectangle."[22] As noted earlier, however, reeds are very pliant. A boat of any size made of such a material will have a flat bottom,

Fig. 43. Naqada I Representation of a Boat: Mosteggeda (After Brunton 1937: pl. 38, and Baumgartel 1955: fig. 21)

Fig. 44. Winkler's Foreign Boat. (After Winkler 1938: fig. 22)

and pulling up and securing the ends of a reed craft will increase its strength and stability. Therefore, since both Egyptians and Mesopotamians built vessels with papyrus and reeds, Winkler's criterion for differentiating the two types of vessels is too general.

Mesopotamian boat representations of the Late Uruk period do exhibit distinguishing features: both ends are high and equal in height or nearly so, both ends curve inward, and a pole is attached to one or both of the curved ends of the craft by two or three ties (figs. 35, 38). Winkler's "foreign boat" thus has little in common with a typical Mesopotamian craft: one end of the foreign boat is considerably higher than the other; one end does curve inward, but the other is vertical; and even though a pole or a rope is attached to the high end of the boat, no ties bind it to the curved end. Therefore, although the square-boat representations published by Winkler bear some similarities to the representations of boats found on Late Uruk cylinder seals, they also manifest attributes that differentiate them from Mesopotamian boats.[23] We may conclude from this that, if the raised end and the pole on Winkler's foreign boat (fig. 44) are indeed inspired by Mesopotamian boats, then, like the master of animals portrayed in the Hierakonpolis mural, they are features that have been almost completely assimilated into Upper Egyptian culture, and, at most, are evidence of indirect contact. Moreover, if these rock drawings do depict Mesopotamian boats, then they, like the high-ended boats on the Gebel el Arak handle, should be relatively free of Egyptian influences, yet none without Egyptian influences exist. In fact, parallels can be discerned when we compare the foreign boat to representations from the Naqada I period (fig. 43) and the Hierakonpolis black boat (fig. 41). Thus, it is possible that this type of craft, with one end considerably higher than the other, is indigenous to Egypt.

The distribution of the rock drawings along the Wadi also casts doubt on Winkler's theory. If it was the corridor through which the "Eastern Invaders" entered Egypt from the Red Sea, then we might expect to find their rock drawings throughout the Wadi's course. Instead, the rock drawing nearest the Red Sea is more than 50 miles inland, and all are in valleys that open into the Nile Valley.[24] Therefore, no evidence associates these drawings directly with the Red Sea.

Numerous studies of Egyptian petroglyphs have been published besides Winkler's work. When all of these publications are compared, it becomes apparent that there is more disagreement than agreement on a practical typology to describe boat petroglyphs and a relative chronology in which to place these vessels.[25] Therefore, a lack of consensus makes it difficult objectively to critique Winkler's typology and chronology. Even if Winkler is correct, however, it is still possible to reconstruct a more likely prehistory of this area using his own data. Winkler divided his drawings into four groups. He labeled their artists Earliest Hunters, Eastern Invaders, Early Nile-Valley Dwellers, and Autochthonous Mountain-Dwellers. He was able to put them in chronological order according to the fauna represented, the superposition and juxtaposition of drawings, and the patination of the drawings. Winkler is aware of the problems involved in dating individual drawings by patination, but he points out that since each group spans such a long period of time, the patination of each drawing can be assigned a relative value, with the number 0 representing the heaviest patination and 10 the lightest.[26]

The earliest of Winkler's four groups is labeled the Earliest Hunters. Representations of elephant, giraffe, and crocodile are common, while antelope, gazelle, Barbary sheep, ibex, and ostrich are rare. The hunters use a large C-shaped bow and possibly nets and game-traps for hunting. Spirals, wavy lines, and intertwined lines are common. Boat representations are unknown. Drawings from this group are always covered by drawings from one of the other three groups. Further, this group of drawings has the heaviest patination, with Winkler giving it a 0–3 rating.[27]

The Earliest Hunters are followed by the Eastern Invaders. Representations of fauna include elephant, hippopotamus, giraffe, ibex, antelope, Barbary sheep, wild cattle, wild ass, ostrich, lizard, dog, and possibly stag and lion. Men commonly wear a headdress of long feathers, and are usually naked, but sometimes wear a kilt; some drawings also suggest that they wore an animal's tail hanging down the back. Women wear long skirts down to their ankles. Weapons shown are a small C-shaped bow, a spiked wheel-trap, a lasso for catching cattle, and, depicted only once, a pear-shaped macehead. Most boats used are the square boat types (figs. 44, 45). Based on the large number of drawings from this group, the Eastern Invaders must have remained in the area for a considerable time. Winkler rated the patination of their drawings from 3 to 4.[28]

This second group appears to be followed by the Early Nile-Valley Dwellers. Representations of fauna include hippopotamus, ibex, antelope, Barbary sheep, wild cattle, domesticated ass, ostrich, crocodile, and some type of feline. The people wear small feathers on their heads, and, in most cases, no clothing is indicated, although a few representations depict men wearing penis sheaths. Weapons

Fig. 45. Square Boat. (After Winkler 1938: fig. 48)

are rare, but one drawing portrays the use of a C-shaped bow. Other drawings indicate the employment of the harpoon, whip, stick and oblong shield, and the lasso for catching cattle. Representations of boats are most abundant in this group. Winkler classifies them as incurved-square boats, incurved-sickle boats, and sickle boats (figs. 46–48). The incurved-square boats were also used by the preceding Eastern Invaders. According to Winkler, the absence of fighting scenes, the scarcity of hunting scenes, and the abundance of boat scenes indicate that these people may have come to the desert for religious reasons. He rated the patination of these representations from 5 to 6.[29]

Winkler's final group, the Autochthonous Mountain-Dwellers, appears to be primarily concerned with cattle breeding. They wear penis sheaths and short kilts; they use a long, double-curved bow, and sometimes a spiked wheel-trap as well. Boat representations are rare; one or two examples of sickle boats are known. It appears that this group lived at the same time as did the Eastern Invaders and the

Fig. 46. Incurved-Square Boat. (After Winkler 1938: fig. 30)

Fig. 47. Incurved-
Sickle Boat.
(After Winkler
1938: fig. 24)

Early Nile-Valley Dwellers, according to the patination rating of 3–6 assigned to the group.[30]

A comparison of the elements in the first three drawing groups suggests that, instead of being intrusive, it is more likely that the Eastern Invaders were indigenous and evolved from the Earliest Hunters and were the forefathers of the Early Nile-Valley Dwellers. All three groups appear to have used a similar type of bow. Like the Earliest Hunters, the Eastern Invaders are shown hunting elephant, giraffe, and crocodile, but smaller game such as antelope, ibex, and gazelle became more important. By the time of the Early Nile-Valley Dwellers, scenes of hunting and fighting had all but disappeared.

Boat representations from the period of the Earliest Hunters are not known to exist, but by the time of the Eastern Invaders, boat drawings are common. The square-boat drawings may represent papyrus boats. The appearance of incurved-square boats could be an indication that wooden vessels were being built, with some of the characteristics of papyrus boats being retained. The incurved-square boats are also used by the Early Nile-Valley Dwellers. According to Winkler, during the period of the Early Nile-Valley Dwellers, incurved-sickle

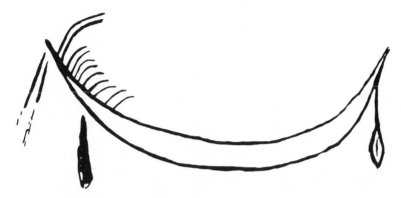

Fig. 48. Sickle Boat.
(After Winkler
1938: fig. 6)

boats and sickle boats appear. These four types of boats may depict the evolution of early Egyptian watercraft, from the papyrus boat (square-boat) to incurved-square boat, then incurved-sickle boats, and, finally, sickle boats. The abundance of boats and lack of hunting scenes during this last period suggest that trade and fishing had replaced hunting as a way of life.

Aside from the similarity of their watercraft and bows, the Eastern Invaders and the Early Nile-Valley Dwellers both wore feathers on their heads. There appears to be a pattern of evolution connecting the three groups. This pattern is supported by the degree of patination that each group exhibited. The primary point of this review is that my evaluation of the Gebel el Arak knife, the Hierakonpolis mural, and the rock drawings suggests that no evidence exists to support the belief that Sumerians traded with Egyptians via the Red Sea. The Nile appears to be a more likely part of the route connecting Upper Egypt to Mesopotamia. This conclusion will be supported by an examination of the Narmer palette.

10 THE NARMER PALETTE

The Narmer palette is both one of the most impressive works of art and one of the most important documents to survive from the close of the Predynastic period (figs. 49 and 50). There are, however, three opposing views as to the historical meaning of the palette's seven registers. The traditional interpretation is that all registers are devoted to the subjugation of the Delta and the unification of Egypt.[1] This explication is opposed both by Yigael Yadin, who proposes that each register "is clearly dedicated to the description of one subject only,"[2] and W. A. Fairservis, Jr., who proposes that all seven registers comprise a document that records a victory by a leader of the Edfu district over peoples of the Nile Valley in southern Upper Egypt and northern Nubia.[3] I will attempt to clarify the opposing views.

The top registers on both sides of the palette are decorated with a pair of goddesses that have a human face, bovine ears, and horns that are carved at each extremity with Narmer's name in the center framed by a *serekh*. These bovine goddesses represent either Hathor or Bat.[4] Henry Fischer proposes that the goddess Hathor supplanted an older crocodile god in the sixth nome in Upper Egypt and, at an early date, became associated with and then assimilated Bat, the goddess of the seventh nome. He continues by arguing that the little evidence that exists suggests that these early cow goddesses on the Narmer Palette are in fact Bat.[5] In contrast, C. J. Bleeker proposes that Hathor, as a cow goddess, derived her bovine qualities from the wild cows that lived in the marshy areas of the Delta, and she may have been the goddess of the third nome of the Delta.[6] The only parallel to this dual cow-goddess motif depicted on the Narmer palette is an engraving on an ivory plaque recovered from the tomb of

Fig. 49. Narmer Palette, Obverse. (After Quibell 1898: pl. 12, and Pritchard 1969: fig. 297)

King Djer, the second king of the First Dynasty. Two bovine goddesses are depicted on one side of this plaque and on the other is an
inscription that states "Hathor in the marshes of King Djer's city of
Dep (Buto),"[7] suggesting that it is Hathor, not Bat, that appears on
the Narmer palette. Bleeker's interpretation actually complements

Fig. 50. Narmer Palette, Reverse. (After Quibell 1898: pl. 13, and Pritchard 1969: fig. 296)

Fischer's by revealing Hathor's origin before she appears in Upper Egypt and assimilates the goddess Bat.

Turning first to the reverse of the palette, the second register portrays Narmer, wearing the White Crown of Upper Egypt, preparing to smite his kneeling foe with a mace.[8] This foe is generally thought to be the ruler of the Harpoon nome, which during dynastic times was located in the northwestern part of the Delta (fig. 50).[9] In contrast, Fairservis maintains that the chieftain is the ruler of Elephantine. His view is based primarily on the interpretation of the papyrus symbol.

Before Narmer is the falcon-god Horus (i.e. Narmer) who holds a rope that passes through the nose or lip of a human head.[10] This head is attached to a pool or land sign (Sign List, M 8 and N 18)[11] and from the land grow six papyrus plants (fig. 50). Fairservis supports the standard interpretation, which states that these last three symbols or *Ta-mehu* sign can be translated as "the people of the papyrus land,"[12] but he offers another possibility for the location of "papyrus land," which is Elephantine. These six papyrus plants are one of the most thoroughly studied of all pre- and early dynastic pictographs, and it is obvious that these papyrus plants are either a recognizable hieroglyph or a prototype for the clump-of-papyrus sign (Sign List, M 16),[13] which refers to the Delta or the North;[14] the Pyramid Texts and other material support this conclusion.[15] In regard to his interpretation of the Narmer palette, Fairservis states that "care must be taken to identify sources in the Pyramid Texts or other potential sources for Old Kingdom material."[16] Yet he dismisses these same sources and fails to produce any convincing textual evidence to support the location of Elephantine as "papyrus land."[17]

In addition, the possibility that "papyrus land" refers to the Delta is strengthened by the fact that the only other comparable sign from the Predynastic period to this *Ta-mehu* sign appears on the Metropolitan Museum Knife Handle. The *Ta-mehu* sign is located above a clump of papyrus with a bent stem; this sign appears to be a prototype of the "clump of papyrus with buds bent down" sign, which also refers to the Delta (Sign List, M 15). Both of the above symbols are in association with what is believed to be a Lower Egyptian shrine (fig. 37).[18] The evidence, therefore, supports the standard interpretation of the Delta as "papyrus land," and the kneeling figure as the chieftain of the Harpoon nome.

In the third register two naked men with long hair and beards, usually assumed to be dead or fleeing, are depicted. Above each man is a sign that presumably indicates his place of origin.[19] That on the right has been suggested to represent Sais, though with some reservation.[20] It has also been interpreted as a papyrus plant with open umbel and two stalks, signifying a Deltaic tribe that revered it.[21] According to W. Ward, the sign to the left is an oblong fortified enclosure with bastions on all sides (fig. 50). This assertion is based on the bastioned walls found on Libyan and Bull palettes and First Dynasty sealings (figs. 32 and 51).[22]

Some scholars argue that the "fortified enclosure" on the palette represents Memphis,[23] citing as evidence three similar signs symbolizing Memphis on a First Dynasty cylinder seal (fig. 51). The signs on the palette and the seal are equated with the *inb*, or wall sign,[24] and the earliest known name for Memphis is the White Wall (*inb ḥḏ*). This name is believed to describe the wall that surrounded the town, and the *inb ḥḏ* sign was sometimes abbreviated to *inb* or the Wall.[25] Thus, since the *inb* sign is an abbreviation of the early form of the name Memphis, and since the *inb* sign is found on the Narmer palette, the fortified enclosure on the palette must represent Memphis. This is a logical and apparently sound deduction, but it does contain a few flaws.

Fig. 51. First Dynasty Seal: Abydos (After Petrie 1900: pl. 23.41)

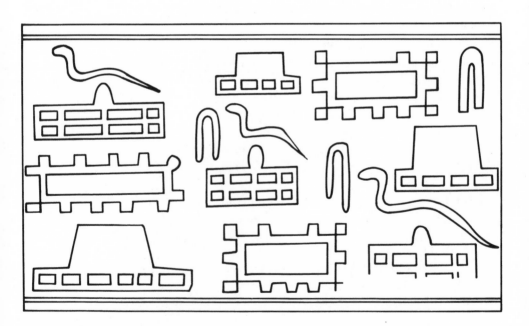

As previously mentioned, the *inb* sign indicates the place of origin of the dead or fleeing figure located below it, but this individual on the palette is believed to be either a foreigner or Lower Egyptian.[26] Therefore, if this *inb* sign is equated with Memphis, then Memphis must have been a foreign or Lower Egyptian settlement at the end of the Naqada III period, but this line of reasoning is not supported by the evidence. As pointed out in Chapter III, Upper Egyptian settlements had replaced Lower Egyptian settlements at least as far north as Minshat Abu Omar in the eastern Delta during the Naqada IIc/d period (fig. 7), and a span of over a hundred years separates the Naqada IIc/d period from the end of the Naqada III period. Therefore, if the *inb* sign does represent Memphis, Memphis must have survived as a foreign or Lower Egyptian settlement long after all other settlements in the region had been vanquished by Upper Egyptians—such a conclusion is baseless.

Another flaw in this argument is that Memphis must have been a major Lower Egyptian site before the subjugation of the Delta. According to tradition, however, Memphis was founded by Menes,[27] the ruler who unified Egypt, and in this instance, archaeological evidence supports tradition. Archaeological material from the First Dynasty is plentiful at Memphis, but nothing has yet been found from the Predynastic period to indicate that Memphis was an important site nor that this site had even been established by Narmer's time.[28] All of the evidence, therefore, indicates that a correlation between the *inb* sign on the Narmer palette and Memphis is unlikely.

The identification of the *inb* sign on the Narmer palette as a fortified enclosure may not be justified either. As noted previously, this interpretation is based only on the similarity of the *inb* sign on the Narmer palette to fortifications portrayed on earlier palettes, but even Ward admits that "in no case do these have precisely the oblong shape of the Narmer palette sign" (figs. 32 and 50).[29] Furthermore, the *inb* sign on the reverse has little in common with the oval-shaped fortress being destroyed by a bull on the obverse (figs. 49 and 50).[30] It seems that if a fortress was to be represented on this palette an oval-shaped fortification sign would have been more appropriate and such a sign is seen on an ebony plaque next to Narmer's name.[31]

In fact, the meaning of the *inb* sign on Narmer's palette is unknown. In the sign list it represents either a fortification or a wall. Although these are standard interpretations for the *inb* sign from the Old and Middle Kingdoms, they do not preclude the possibility that during the Predynastic period this sign may have signified some other type of brick structure with bastions or crenelations, such as a temple, tomb, or palace,[32] which only later evolved into the *inb ḥd* sign that represented Memphis. Gardiner mentions that in earliest times the *inb* sign may have represented a "brick enclosure with buttresslike projections," but he does not say what type of brick enclosure.[33] The fact that the *inb* sign was an element in titles of architects, masons, and master bricklayers of the king also suggests a wider meaning for this sign.[34]

Yadin's opposing interpretation of the third register on the reverse suggests that the two prostrate men are Asiatic enemies. The sign above the man on the right is a representation of a kite, a structure with long converging walls that end in an enclosure (fig. 52). The converging walls were probably used to move herds quickly into the enclosure for protection. As kites were characteristic of the eastern deserts of Jordan, and because fortresses first appeared in Palestine during the Early Bronze I period, Yadin saw the sign on the left as a Palestinian fortress. He proposed that "the lower field of the palette records Narmer's domination of the two main highways between Egypt, Syria and Mesopotamia: the 'sea road' and the 'king's way'. The former cuts through the most fortified part of Palestine,

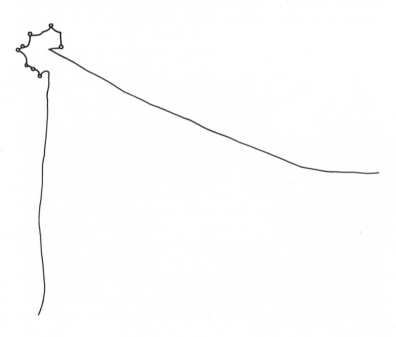

Fig. 52. Kite.
(After Mazar 1990:
fig. 2.11)

the latter through the less inhabited and much less fortified plateau of Transjordan."[35] Since this theory was first presented, kites have been found in the Sinai desert.[36] Based on this information, Samuel Yeivin amended Yadin's interpretation. He maintains that there is no need for any deep Egyptian penetration beyond the confines of the northern Negev.[37] Yeivin attempts to bolster his position by proposing that the peoples represented by the fortress and the kite can be identified with terms from later texts. He suggests that the fortress signifies a sedentary and agriculturally based population known as the *Mntyw*, or "winnowers," and that the kite represents a pastoral, seminomadic people of southern Canaan and possibly the Sinai known as the *hryw-še*, or "those upon the sand."[38] Ward persuasively argues that Yeivin's linguistic analysis is questionable and that Yeivin ignored what would be even more convincing linguistic evidence in constructing his argument.[39] For example, Yeivin derived his interpretation of *Mntyw* as winnowers from a rare verb that may mean to "sieve grain," while ignoring the more common meaning of "wild ones."[40]

Ward proceeds to expose other weaknesses in Yadin and Yeivin's theory of an incursion into Palestine. He agrees that there is a striking resemblance between the two prostrate figures on the Narmer palette and foreigners portrayed on First Dynasty monuments,[41] but in a later publication he cites a study by William Smith that suggests representations of foreigners on predynastic artifacts merely reflect the diverse population that had migrated to the Delta from various locations—not an excursion to a foreign land.[42]

Ward continues by stating that few similarities are shared by the fortress portrayed on the Narmer palette and fortresses found in Palestine during the Early Bronze I period: "Palestinian structures of the period were not strengthened with regular buttresses. They show instead rounded 'towers' at certain points along the wall; . . ."[43] As previously mentioned, this argument is also valid when comparing the fortress on the Narmer palette to representations of Egyptian fortifications on predynastic artifacts. Another flaw in Yadin's argument is that although some walled sites started to appear in Palestine during the Early Bronze Ib period,[44] the large fortifications that he bases his theory on have been re-dated to the Early Bronze II and III periods.[45] Finally, Ward agrees that the structures Yadin calls kites resemble somewhat the sign on the Narmer palette, but he also argues that "both signs on the palette can be identified as hieroglyphs on paleographical grounds, making Yadin's foreign hypothesis unnecessary."[46]

The second register on the obverse of the Narmer palette shows Narmer, wearing the Red Crown, inspecting the decapitated bodies of the enemy (fig. 49). Fairservis interprets this register by describing the sandal-bearer as governor of Edfu and commander of Narmer's troops, who with warships of Neith, beheads the chiefs of the Medja(y) of Nubia.[47] Above the sandal-bearer is a large rectangle containing a triangular-shaped sign. Fairservis proposes that this triangular or reed-float sign (Sign List T 25) within a rectangle refers to the district of Edfu; the district from which the sandal-bearer mounts a campaign to Elephantine and Nubia.[48] The interpretation of this sign as meaning Edfu is based on the possibility that this "reed-float" sign is the first element in the name of Edfu. Even if Edfu is the correct interpretation of this sign, it may have been portrayed in this register because it was a center of the falcon-god Horus,[49] the god who is associated with the king on the reverse of the palette. The reed-float sign is also an element in the word for "chest" which in the texts refers to the "ka of the king."[50] This sign may also be interpreted as a "brick" building[51] or a temple.[52] Thus, the procession may be starting from a building, such as a temple, built of brick in the vanquished town that this register describes. The meaning of this sign is obscure and Fairservis's interpretation is viable, but considering the context of this sign in relation to the palette as a whole, it is probable that this "reed-float" sign indirectly refers to the king or to an important building at Buto.

Fairservis continues by interpreting the bound bodies as being from Medja of Nubia. This view is based solely on the possibility that the bindings securing the arms to the bodies of all ten victims can be related to the hieroglyphic word for "bonds" (𓎛𓂝 𓏤𓏤), which can then be related to the word for the people of Medja (𓈖𓂝𓈖𓂋𓈗).[53] This is at best a tenuous argument. A simpler and more credible interpretation is that the bound bodies are a variant of the sign of "man with arms tied behind his back" (Sign List, A 13), which is a determinative for enemy. Fairservis supports his argument by proposing that the headdresses being worn by nine of these chiefs are suggestive of feathers and help identify "their 'barbaric' and ethnically demonstrative status,"[54] but he fails to cite any Nubian parallels to justify this interpretation. In contrast, Egyptians, possibly from the Delta, are depicted wearing feathered headdresses on the Hunters palette.[55]

The preceding interpretations are the foundation upon which Fair-servis constructs his argument that this palette describes an incursion into Nubia, but his interpretations are weak and ignore more convincing ones.

Above the decapitated bodies is carved a door, a bird, a boat, and a falcon. The "door" sign usually signifies a frontier post or stronghold that controls access into Egypt. For example, a hieroglyph consisting of a door and a sedge refers to the southern frontier post of Elephantine or the "Door of the South".[56] On the Narmer palette, the door sign is translated as the "Great Door" and the falcon is equated with the falcon-god Horus (i.e. Narmer), and the boat signifies the Harpoon nome. This group of symbols has been interpreted to describe Narmer's taking of the Great Door (or Port?) of Buto because a port at Buto would control access to the sea.[57] The king and his entourage therefore are proceeding through Buto to inspect the decapitated bodies of his enemy (fig. 49).

The third register portrays two panthers or lions with long, entwined necks; both animals are leashed and each is being restrained by one man. Felines with long necks are found on other palettes, but the closest parallel to the long-necked felines on the Narmer palette comes from a Mesopotamian cylinder seal (figs. 49, 53), a seal that may be Syrian in origin.[58] On the Narmer palette the entwined necks of the animals have been interpreted as symbolizing the unification of northern and southern Egypt[59] and, because of the two leashes restraining them, the subjugation of a people.[60] The primary difficulty with this idea is that no one has explained why a Mesopotamian motif was chosen to express either sentiment. Yadin, the only scholar

Fig. 53. Mesopotamian Seal with Serpent-Necked Felines: Unknown (Detail after Collon 1987: fig. 885)

to try, noted the strong Mesopotamian affinities and proposed that the two intertwined necks represented the Tigris and Euphrates rivers; he formulated an Egyptian incursion into Mesopotamia to explain this obvious connection between Egypt and Mesopotamia.[61]

In the fourth register of the obverse is a bull, which signifies the power of the king, trampling an enemy and demolishing the walls of a fortress. The fortress encloses a trapezoidal structure with inverted triangles at either end. Yeivin notes a resemblance between this sign and one inside a fortress on the Tjehenu (or Libyan) palette (fig. 32). The upraised arms on the Tjehenu palette are believed to be the ka sign ( ). On the reverse of that palette, in the bottom register, is a pictograph of a throwing stick, a sign designating Libya in standard hieroglyphs. Based on these two signs from the Tjehenu palette, Yeivin suggests that the fourth register on the Narmer palette's obverse commemorates a victory over a fortified town on the Libyan borderland.[62] One problem with this theory is that we do not know if the Libya represented by the throwing stick on the Tjehenu palette is the Libya of dynastic times. Yeivin accepts the possibility that part of Libya may have been assimilated into the northwest Delta in predynastic times.[63] P. E. Newberry interprets the throwing stick sign to mean "olive-land." He states that in early times, "olive-land included the Mareotis lake region and all the country to the west of the Canopic branch of the Nile, possibly also *much of the Delta itself.*"[64] When we consider, however, that both the Tjehenu and Narmer palettes are believed to be roughly contemporary[65] and considering the distribution of Upper Egyptian settlements at this time (figs. 6 and 7), it is unlikely that Tjehenu extended any farther east than the site of Minshat Abu Omar nor any farther south than the apex of the Delta, and, so far, no predynastic settlements west of the Delta have been discovered that can be equated with the signs inscribed on this palette, suggesting that Tjehenu was located in the western Delta.

Finally, the ka sign on the Tjehenu palette, which Yeivin equates with the trapezoidal design with two inverted triangles on the Narmer palette, has also been interpreted to represent Sais.[66] In contrast, Siegfried Schott points out that the beetle, papyrus, and ka were all worshipped in Buto and, since Buto was the religious capital of the Delta, all of the enclosed signs on the Tjehenu palette depict the gods worshipped at Buto.[67] Consequently, it seems quite possible that the Tjehenu palette depicts a raid against Lower Egyptian settlements at some location west of Minshat Abu Omar in the Delta, or possibly against Buto, and that the destroyed fortress on the Narmer palette represents either Sais or Buto.

This foregoing review demonstrates clearly that the traditional interpretation of the Narmer palette as recording a final triumph over Lower Egypt, even with its flaws, is the stronger of the three arguments, but two other interpretations have been proposed that argue against any historical interpretation. The first is by N. B. Millet, who believes that the signs on the Narmer palette, and those also on the Narmer and Scorpion maceheads, merely represent year names used to date the year when an object was made and presented to a temple. A year name describes an event in the year of a king's reign. These events include military campaigns, religious festivals, and even rather commonplace occurences. Millet's argument is based in large part on the belief that the scenes on all three objects must be regarded as precise inscriptions instead of simple pictorial renderings of events.[68] For the scenes on these three artifacts to represent precise year names as Millet proposes suggests that such inscriptions were the result of a long period of development and that the practice of inscribing year names on gifts was well established during the Late Predynastic period. Millet supports his argument by pointing out that royal tablets dating to the First and Second Dynasties and stone vases from Hierakonpolis dating to the late Second Dynasty all bear year names.[69] A major flaw in Millet's argument is that he fails to cite any evidence that year names were used before the time of Narmer or Scorpion.

If Millet is correct and the Narmer palette is inscribed with only a year name, then the same should be true for earlier inscribed objects, such as other predynastic palettes and knife handles. Although a number of palettes have survived, Millet fails to cite any of the scenes on these palettes, or any other predynastic objects, to show how year names evolved into the precise and elaborate inscriptions that appear on the Narmer palette, macehead, and Scorpion macehead. If these objects are engraved with only year names, then we would expect to see similar year names engraved on stone containers or other valuable items dating to the First Dynasty, but Millet fails to cite any such evidence. The "royal tablets" that Millet cites are crudely carved ivory and wood tags for identifying and dating various goods.[70] Millet's argument is weakened by his failure to show any continuity connecting these late predynastic "year names" with earlier and later examples or by showing any continuity in the practice of engraving any predynastic or early First Dynasty offerings with year names.

Millet's argument is supported primarily on the premise that the scenes that appear on the Narmer palette, macehead, and Scorpion macehead can all be translated as precise year names. He supports his position by showing that each sign on the Narmer macehead has a specific meaning and that they can be translated together as "Year of the Festival of Appearance of the King of Lower Egypt; (First Occasion of) Counting."[71] If his premise has any validity, we would expect that each of the signs on the Narmer palette are as significant as those on the Narmer macehead, making it possible to derive specific year names from the signs in each register on the Narmer palette. Yet, Millet has little success in his translation of these registers. He states that the smiting scene on the palette should be translated "as something like 'Year of Smiting the Northland'." He concedes that the second register on the obverse of the palette "is not easily to be matched by any of the kinds of events used to form year-names on the Palermo stone or the Archaic tablets." He feels that this scene can "only be explained as a continuation and elaboration of the theme or event depicted on the front." He believes that the year name in this register has only one essential element, which suggests that the other signs are superfluous. The bottom register on the reverse side depicting a bull battering down a fortress is translated as the year name of "Opening up . . . the Fortress Such and Such."[72] The remainder of the registers are for the most part ignored. Instead of producing a document in which the scenes in each register represent a precise interpretation, Millet abandons this aspect of his argument and relies on rather vague and general translations. In effect, the iconography on the Narmer palette appears to be too elaborate to represent merely year names as proposed by Millet.

The Narmer palette and Scorpion macehead are two of the most sophisticated works of art from the Predynastic period. The scenes on both objects are far more elaborate than would be expected for a gift bearing only a year name. If these objects were in fact inscribed to celebrate actual events, they probably evolved from earlier depictions and engravings such as the Hierakonpolis mural, the Gebel el Arak handle and predynastic palettes. In contrast, written forms of year names are bureaucratic and informal and probably developed as an aid to administration.[73] The use of year names probably evolved from the simple markings such as those seen on the ivory plaques and painted on pottery from Tomb U-j, which were an aid to identifying and accounting for grave goods.[74] Names engraved on stone vases and bowls and the use of ivory and wood tags during late predynastic times reflects a continuation of this practice. During the beginning of the First Dynasty, ivory and wooden labels become more elaborate and record events in the reign of the king, but they were still used as labels to designate oil jars and other goods.[75] By the middle of the First Dynasty, during the reign of King Den, the year sign *rnpt* is added to labels indicating a more complex system of administration than in previous reigns.[76] Even the Palermo stone, on which Millet bases most of his interpretations, contains registers for inundation levels that were probably used to calculate taxes suggesting that this document was meant as an aid to administration.[77] Egyptian writing evolved by being used to perform administrative, religious, and political functions. Year names may, therefore, be a type of administrative shorthand derived from both the elaborate scenes on commemorative objects, such as the Narmer palette, and simpler tags used to designate goods, which were to more precisely account for an increasing number of goods being produced by a society that was rapidly growing more complex. At the same time, the elaborate scenes on artifacts like the Narmer palette expressed the political and religious ideology of the ruling hierarchy and provided the basis of Egyptian literature, such as the Pyramid Texts. To propose that early Egyptian writing is made up merely of tags and year names would reflect a rather materialistic society and such a society is not represented by the archaeological evidence.

The second interpretation of the Narmer palette is proposed by John Baines, who agrees that the scenes on the Narmer palette do seem to refer to specific people, events, and places and describe an internal victory of south over north. He agrees that "papyrus land" should signify the Delta, but argues that the Delta had been part of a unified Egyptian state for generations by the time of Narmer. He proposes that the authentic detail on this palette is derived from traditional sources, such as early narratives dating to the Naqada IIIa period, which depict the peoples who were defeated in the unification of the country.[78] If this explanation were correct it would seem that portrayals of the unification of Egypt would be popular among the kings of the Naqada III period, but the Narmer palette is in fact the earliest example of such a scene. In contrast, scenes of warfare are rather common at this time.

Baines bases this interpretation on the belief that Egypt was po-
litically unified as early as the Naqada IIIa period. His interpretation
is based partly on a few royal symbols recovered from Tomb U-j at
Abydos. These symbols consist of an ivory scepter in the shape of a
crook and bone or ivory labels possibly attached to bolts of cloth, of
which one was decorated with a "palace-facade" motif. The evidence
that the occupant of this tomb ruled over a unified Egypt consists
of a few bone labels that may be inscribed with the name of Buto
or Bubastis.[79]

In regard to the evidence for political unity, the labels attached
to the bolts of cloth in Tomb U-j may be the result of trade with
Bubastis or Buto. This is supported by the large amount of Palestinian pottery recovered from the tomb, which may be the result of
wealth derived from new Deltaic trade centers, like Minshat Abu
Omar. Tomb U-j undoubtably housed the remains of an early king,
but whether he was a regional king or a king that may have ruled as
far north as Minshat Abu Omar is unknown.

Baines concedes that the royal symbols found in Tomb U-j dif-
fered significantly from those of the First Dynasty, and that no real
proof exists to show that this early king ruled over all of Egypt. He
bases his belief of an early unification on what he perceives as a cultural unity throughout Egypt. He argues that this cultural unity begins as early as the Naqada IIc/d period with the replacement of
Lower Egyptian sites by Upper Egyptian sites, as seen at Minshat
Abu Omar in the Delta, and is completed with the fall of Buto. A
transitional layer in which local Lower Egyptian pottery is replaced
by Upper Egyptian pottery is cited as evidence of the conquest of
Buto. This transition occurred before the unification of Egypt and is
seen as evidence that Buto had become a Naqada site under the control of the kings of Abydos.[80]

A number of difficulties are inherent in this argument. As previously mentioned, other Lower Egyptian sites are suddenly replaced
by Upper Egyptian sites not slowly assimilated like Buto. This break
in the pattern raises some doubt as to the validity of interpreting this
change in pottery styles as evidence of a conquest. Thomas von der
Way explains this transition by speculating that a chieftain from Upper Egypt siezed control of Lower Egypt, but, because of the presumed importance of Buto, killed only the ruling class, after which
the commoners were slowly assimilated into the new culture.[81] It
would seem that logic would dictate an opposite response; a site

as important as Buto, or any important site, can best be secured by quickly removing the vanquished population, especially since the people to be replaced appear to have lacked necessary or unique skills. So far, no archaeological evidence suggests a population short-age in Upper Egypt that would make it difficult to replace the indige-nous people of Buto.

It is possible to produce more than one interpretion of this tran-sition from Lower Egyptian to Upper Egyptian pottery. This transi-tion begins with the appearance of some Naqada pottery styles, but Lower Egyptian pottery types are dominant in the archaeological re-cord and all pottery is made using Lower Egyptian techniques con-sisting of fabrics with greater amounts of chaff and straw and low firing temperatures. These techniques are replaced by fabrics and higher firing temperatures used in Upper Egypt, but even though Upper Egyptian techniques have been adopted, most pottery types are still Lower Egyptian. Finally, Upper Egyptian styles replace all but a few Lower Egyptian types that may have survived to the end of the Predynastic period.[82] When we take into account the early at-tempts to copy Upper Egyptian pottery at Maadi, this transition may indicate nothing more than the close proximity of Buto to new Na-qada sites in the Delta that gave the inhabitants of Buto greater access to Upper Egyptian pottery types followed by access to the tech-niques used to make this pottery. If Buto was actually captured, we would expect that new pottery styles, fabrics, and firing techniques would have been introduced at the same time.

Another difficulty with this argument is that pottery is only one aspect of culture. If Baines is correct, then we should see few cultural differences between Buto and other Naqada sites after the tansitional period. In regard to architecture this does not appear to be true; evi-dence for the Lower Egyptian practice of decorating walls with clay cones is more plentiful after the period of transition than before and continues until the early third millenium,[83] while we lack evidence for this practice at other Naqada sites. Based on the published evi-dence, it is impossible to show that Buto was transformed into a Na-qada site at the end of the Naqada II period.

In contrast, it is possible to reconstruct the Naqada IIc/d and Naqada III periods as a time of passage to unification. The replace-ment of Lower Egyptian sites by Upper Egyptian sites during the Naqada IIc/d period marks the beginning of the Upper Egyptian expansion into the Delta. The increasing size of the tombs in cemetery B at Abydos represents the wealth generated by such expansion through war and trade. Continued warfare between Upper Egyptian and western Deltaic sites is portrayed on numerous knife handles and palettes, such as the Tjehenu palette which possibly depicts raids against the Kingdom of Buto. This constant portrayal of war seems to end with the "unification of Egypt" depicted on the Narmer palette. Furthermore, the widespread appearance of King Narmer's name throughout Egypt and Palestine suggests unprecedented influence. As Baines points out the architectural remains of the tombs from the Late Predynastic period are neither impressive nor very large;[84] such tombs could have easily been supported by a regional economy. In contrast, at the beginning of the First Dynasty, Neith-hotep's tomb at Naqada and the large crenelated tombs at Saqqara are the earliest physical evidence of monumental construction beyond the ability and resources of regional kingdoms. Narmer's reign is succeeded by a period of unprecedented stratification of Egyptian society, the appearance of a centralized state economy, and the establishment of a new capital at Memphis. The magnitude of changes in such a short period suggests that some event during Narmer's reign was pivotal in the transition of Egyptian culture to becoming a state. This event may have been the fall of the last of the Lower Egyptian kingdoms. Such an event would have introduced a period of stability. Resources for war could be diverted to other works. Acquisition of the Port of Buto would supply a new source of wealth that is represented by an unprecedented increase in the appearance of Syrian goods in Egyptian tombs.[85] We cannot, therefore, rely solely on arguments of iconography to dismiss the possibility that the Narmer palette celebrates a historical event. Although the process of unifying Egypt took much longer than originally thought, a political unification of Egypt is still best marked by the scenes depicted on the Narmer palette, which led to the rise of the Egyptian state at the beginning of the First Dynasty.

If the Narmer palette does indeed portray the unification of Egypt, then a few amendments make plausible a variation of the traditional interpretation that may explain the flaws described above. This variation is predicated on the possibility that Buto was the main port through which Mesopotamian influences entered Egypt.[86]

The top register on both sides of the palette are decorated with Narmer's name in the center framed by a *serekh* and a pair of goddesses that represent Hathor. Hathor's name is usually translated as the "House of Horus." She is described as a warrior goddess,[87] and this aspect of Hathor's character is in agreement with the overall subject of the Narmer palette. As previously mentioned, the earliest indication of Hathor comes from an ivory plaque dating to the reign of King Djer, which affiliates Hathor with Buto. This early association with Buto may have resulted in her becoming protector of shipping to foreign parts. She is also identified with the mother goddess at Byblos, the patroness of shipmasters. According to Bleeker, this relationship is due to early trading between Egypt and Syria.[88]

It is now necessary to review the interpretation of the smiting scene in the second register on the reverse of the palette (fig. 50), the closest parallel to which is the smiting scene on the Hierakonpolis mural (fig. 54). The smiter stands before three bound prisoners while holding his mace at the base of the handle. In contrast, on the Narmer palette, Narmer holds his mace closer to the macehead than to the base of the handle, more like a trophy than a weapon. Also, unlike the Hierakonpolis mural the captive is not bound. That the prisoners on the Hierakonpolis mural are bound suggests that the captives still pose a threat. The absence of bonds on Narmer's captive seems to indicate that even though Narmer is holding his weapon in neither a

Fig. 54. Smiting Scene from the Hierakonpolis Mural. (Detail after Quibell and Green 1902: pl. 75)

threatening nor a defensive manner, the now former ruler has been so completely crushed that he is no longer a threat. This is not only a portrayal of domination but also of humiliation.

According to the standard interpretation, the grasping of each captive by the hair is seen on both the Hierakonpolis mural and the Narmer palette,[89] but the Hierakonpolis mural lacks the detail necessary to show any hair, and, instead, the warrior appears to be holding a rope that binds the three prisoners (fig. 54).[90] On the Narmer palette, the "hair" that rests on Narmer's hand may in fact be a cylinder seal. This object has a shape reminiscent of a cylinder seal, it rests on the back of his hand instead of being centered over the fist as we would expect a knot of hair held in his grasp to be, and a faint incision across Narmer's wrist suggests a strap to hold such a seal.[91] This interpretation is supported by the lack of incisions on this object. The artist who carved this palette produced a meticulously detailed work of art, including hair. It seems unlikely that if the carver wished to create a clump of hair, he would have neglected to add the wavy lines seen on the head of the kneeling chieftain and on all of the other heads depicted on the palette. Considering the details lavished on other objects in the same register, the addition of such lines appears easily within the abilities of the artist; the seal can best be differentiated from the hair by a lack of adornment. Finally, the possibility has been raised that the figure standing behind Narmer is in fact the bearer of the king's cylinder seal.[92] A cylinder seal may, therefore, be part of the royal regalia worn by Narmer.

A similar representation portraying a king holding pieces of the royal regalia in both hands is depicted on an ivory label dating to the reign of Den, the fourth king of the First Dynasty. The king stands above his kneeling enemy with a mace in his right hand, and his left hand rests on the head of his victim, and in it he grasps a long pole or "staff of office" and what appears to be a rope.[93] This "rope" is usually described as a lock of hair,[94] but, unlike the victim's hair, it is considerably longer and the hatching pattern suggests that, unlike the hair of the captive, it is tied off near the end—as is done with a piece of rope (fig. 55). The other end of the rope appears to be represented by a line behind the victim's beard. This line cannot be the base of the neck because it should have an orientation similar to the lines that define the shoulders; instead, one end of this line is considerably higher than the other, suggesting a rope being pulled upwards. Also, the posture of the victim, the location of the knee above the

Fig. 55. Smiting Scene of King Den: Abydos (Detail after Spencer 1993, fig. 67)

ground, and the awkward placement of the hands on the leg and near the fist of the king is more consistent with someone being strangled with a rope than merely having the king grasp a lock of hair. The practice of tying a rope around a captives neck is seen on an engraved slip of ivory dating roughly to Narmer's time,[95] and the earliest parallel to a bound captive in a smiting scene is depicted on the Hierakonpolis mural where all three kneeling prisoners are bound with a rope. Early smiting scenes lack evidence for the grasping of hair but do contain evidence of the king holding pieces of his regalia in both hands above his vanquished foe.

Another important aspect of this scene is the White Crown Narmer wears. In dynastic times the White Crown was the insignia of Upper Egyptian royalty while the Red Crown was associated with Lower Egypt.[96] Curiously, the Red Crown first appears on a fragment of Upper Egyptian pottery recovered at Naqada that dates from the Naqada Id to IIa periods,[97] and a Susan cylinder seal dating

Fig. 56. Susan Seal Depicting a White Crown? (Detail after Amiet 1961: fig. 282)

as early as the Late Uruk period (fig. 56) may bear the earliest White Crown.[98] One of the earliest representations of the White Crown in Egyptian art is found on the Metropolitan Museum knife handle, where a king wears the crown while seated in a high-ended, Mesopotamian-style vessel. The similarities between this vessel and the high-ended ones on the Gebel el Arak handle are obvious, including the pole bearing the crescent insignia (figs. 34, 37, and 56). This crescent insignia does not seem to have any close parallels in predynastic Egyptian art, but a similar one is evident on the Susan cylinder seal mentioned earlier. The crescent insignia is attached to a pole and is located behind the man wearing the White Crown on both the Metropolitan Museum knife handle and the Susan cylinder seal (figs. 37 and 56). Thus, it seems possible that the White Crown was originally a Susan or Mesopotamian headdress that became part of the royal regalia of Lower Egypt.

This view is supported by a comparison of the hair of the vanquished ruler with the hair of the disembodied head in the same register and the hair of the two men in the third register. The lines that represent the hair of the three smaller figures are essentially consistent in spacing throughout their length. In contrast, the lines below the headband of the vanquished ruler are quite widely spaced in relation to those above the headband (figs. 49 and 50). If these lines do indeed depict hair, why is it so crudely rendered on one of the largest heads on the palette while the hair on smaller heads is so finely executed? Perhaps the lines below the headband depict not hair but the lower part of a headdress—a headdress that remained after the crown of the former ruler was plucked from his head by Narmer.

If this interpretation of the second register is correct, we would expect the White Crown to appear in Upper Egyptian art at approximately the time of or later than the unification of Egypt. The only artifacts dating to the Predynastic period that bear the White Crown are the Narmer palette and macehead, the Scorpion macehead, the Metropolitan Museum knife handle, and the Qustul and Archaic Horus incense burners. With the exception of the Narmer palette and macehead, the dating of these items is in question and a review of each, starting with the Scorpion macehead, may clarify the problem.

The largest figure and central scene on the Scorpion macehead portrays a king holding a hoe and wearing a simple tunic and the White Crown. This figure is facing two signs, a rosette and a scorpion (fig. 57). The standard interpretation is that the rosette and scorpion represent the name of King Scorpion, supposedly Narmer's predecessor.[99] The rosette, in effect, replaces the *serekh* to designate the king. This interpretation, however, is flawed. The *serekh* encloses Narmer's name on both the Narmer palette and macehead, and, considering that the Scorpion macehead is roughly contemporary with both of these artifacts,[100] the use of the *serekh* appears to be an established convention at this time, and so far no credible interpretation has been proposed to explain the replacement of the *serekh* by a rosette in this context. Another flaw is that we lack other examples of a rosette being used to signify a king. The belief that the rosette is equated with the king appears to be based solely on the use of the rosette to designate the sandal or cylinder-seal bearers as royal servants on the Narmer palette and macehead. The difficulty with this line of reasoning is that of all known examples of the rosette it is only on the Scorpion macehead that it signifys the king. Moreover, if the rosette was used to designate the king, like the *serekh*, the placement of a rosette on the Scorpion macehead appears to be redundant because the king wears the White Crown which signifies his position. The same context is seen in the second register on the obverse of the Narmer palette. Narmer is depicted wearing the Red crown and in front of him are the chisel and catfish signs that signify his name, but without being enclosed in a *serekh* as in the first register. In this scene

Fig. 57. King Scorpion?: Hierakonpolis (Detail after Quibell 1900, pl. 26c.4)

the *serekh* appears to be unnecessary because Narmer is wearing a crown, making it rather obvious to the viewer that he is the king.

Harry Smith has proposed that the rosette comes originally from Susa or southern Mesopotamia where it was used to signify divine heroes or kings and as such can be associated with the kingship in Egypt,[101] but the interpretations on which he constructs his argument are questionable. For example, he proposes that in the motif consisting of two intertwined snakes and three rosettes (fig. 19), the rosettes symbolize the triumph of the hero, and the snakes are equated with a vanquished darkness and evil,[102] but he ignores the standard and more convincing interpretation that the intertwined snakes are copulating and are a fertility symbol.[103]

Below the rosette on the macehead is a scorpion which is believed to signify the king's name (fig. 57). Those that support this interpretation have failed to explain the significance of the shaft that protrudes from the belly of the scorpion. We lack examples of this combination of a sign and a shaft being used to signify a person's name. In contrast, such a combination appears to be more consistent with some type of a standard or title, possibly signifying a clan or god,[104] and this sign is also considered a sign of good luck.[105] If the scorpion sign is indeed the name of a king, the rosette should be included as part of his name and not as a title, and the shaft must be explained.

Two other difficulties are present in accepting the existence of a King Scorpion: the first is a lack of consensus concerning Scorpion's chronological placement, especially since he is placed before and after Narmer,[106] and the second is a paucity of archaeological evidence that indicates such a king ever existed. It has been claimed that his name appears on a few other objects, but these interpretations are problematical.[107] The existence of such a king is based almost solely on the interpretation of the two signs on this macehead.

Elise Baumgartel proposes that this macehead portrays Narmer, and the rosette and scorpion signs represent a goddess instead of a name. According to Baumgartel the rosette and scorpion signs are Mesopotamian religious symbols; the rosette is a common fertility symbol and may signify a mother-goddess, and the scorpion, Selket, is associated with motherhood and protection. For example, Isis and her son Horus were protected by scorpions as they hid in the Deltaic marshes near Buto.[108] Baumgartel believes that this scene portrays Narmer participating in a foundation ceremony for a temple to Horus. The goddess signified by the rosette and scorpion are a counterpart to Horus, and she brings good luck to the ceremony by her presence. The main weakness in her argument is a lack of a parallel for representing a goddess in this fashion.

The main difficulty with both of the above interpretations is that we have too little information to do more than guess as to the meaning of these two symbols, and, as such, these signs are of little value in helping to date this object. The most effective way of dating the Scorpion macehead is by studying the style and quality of workmanship. This macehead, the Narmer palette, and Narmer macehead all appear to have been sculpted not only at the same time and place, but possibly from the hand of the same master sculptor.[109] Even if the rosette and scorpion signs do translate as King Scorpion, the most recent chronological interpretation places this king between Narmer and Aha. The evidence indicates that the Scorpion mace-head is contemporary with or later than the Narmer palette.

In regard to the iconography on the Metropolitan Museum handle, the high-ended and sickle-shaped vessels on it have obvious parallels with the vessels on the Gebel el Arak handle, but there are also differences between the representations on both objects. The Gebel el Arak handle illustrates a battle between the people of the sickle boats and those of the high-ended boats. Based upon similarities shared by the master-of-animals motif on this handle and on the Hierakonpolis mural, this handle probably dates to the end of the Naqada II period or beginning of the Naqada III period.[110] In contrast, the Metropolitan Museum handle relates a victory celebration that includes both types of vessels. This handle also exhibits a papyrus plant with one bent stem and a Lower Egyptian shrine, both of which are found on the Scorpion macehead, and a king seated in a boat wearing the White Crown, which is also found on the Qustul and Archaic Horus incense burners, and the *Ta-mehu* sign appears on both the Metropolitan Museum knife handle and the Narmer palette.[111] The rosette in association with the White Crown appears on the Metropolitan Museum knife handle, the Narmer palette, the Scorpion macehead, and the Qustul incense burner. Finally, according to B. Williams and T. J. Logan, the images on both the knife handle and the Narmer palette are devoted to two general themes: a victory on one side and a sacrifice on the other.[112] Therefore, based on the iconopgraphy, all of these objects should be considered contemporary with the Narmer palette. The only difficulty with this interpretation is that the incense burners are dated to the Naqada IIIa period,[113] but their published date appears dubious.

Williams states that the two incense burners are approximately contemporary, but that the Qustul incense burner is believed to be somewhat earlier.[114] This date is, therefore, crucial to this discussion. The Qustul incense burner comes from Cemetery L in Nubia, some pottery from which appears to be firmly dated to the Naqada III period.[115] Williams proposes a linear seriation for most of the tombs in Cemetery L, listing tomb L 24, the tomb that contains the Qustul incense burner, as one of the earliest in his chronology, and dating it to the Naqada IIIa1 period.[116]

The primary evidence for dating tomb L 24 to the Naqada IIIa1 period consists of a fragment of a pot with a transversely elongated body, a group of Palestinian jugs,[117] and a segmented jar.[118] The pottery fragment and segmented jar are of the Naqada IIIa period, but the dating of the Palestinian jugs is less certain. The closest parallel for the jugs comes from a tomb at Azor, which is assigned by Williams to no later than Naqada IIIa on the basis of a ripple-flaked knife found in the tomb.[119] The excavation report reveals, however, that this tomb is thought to have been used for only a short period of time, that the partial remains of the knife were unearthed with the Palestinian jugs, and that the excavator believes the knife to have been an heirloom when it was interred in the tomb. The tomb is therefore dated not by the knife blade, but by a number of Egyptian and Palestinian objects, including pottery, to ca. 3100 B.C.[120]

Other pottery in tomb L 24 comprise in part the remains of possibly seven pot-stands of at least three types. Two of the stands are low and plain. Two others are high with incised decorations around their rims and rectangular openings on their sides. Fragments of three other stands, two of which had triangular openings on their sides, were also recovered.[121] The low stands appear in Egypt during the Naqada IIIa period,[122] but the literature seems to indicate that they are rare throughout the Naqada III period and do not become common until the First Dynasty.[123] The tall stands appear to be rather common in the early dynasties, but may date as early as the end of the Naqada III period.[124] Therefore, the pottery stands in this tomb support a First Dynasty date.

One stone vessel, a portion of another, and some beads were also found in tomb L 24. The partial vessel is the upper half of a cylinder jar with wavy bands; a shallow bowl with a flat base is intact. According to Williams, the cylinder jar could have been produced in Egypt during the Naqada III period through the First Dynasty,[125] but the shallow bowl was produced only during the First Dynasty.[126] He contends that some cylinder jars and stone bowls must be redated from the First Dynasty to the Naqada IIIa period to account for their appearance in the Cemetery L tombs.[127] With regard to the beads, Williams cites as parallels only the "early versions of the grooved pendant and of the bilobate beads . . . found among the jewelry deposited in the [First Dynasty] tomb of Djer."[128]

In order to date tomb L 24 to the Naqada IIIa period, it is necessary to push back to the Naqada IIIa period, from as late as the First Dynasty, the earliest accepted dates for some stone bowls and tall, decorated pot-stands,[129] and to accept the possibility that both low and high pot-stands were commonly used significantly earlier than the evidence suggests. It also requires acceptance of a theory proposed by Williams concerning a mummified arm that was recovered from the tomb of Djer.

Williams speculates that this arm was stolen from a Naqada IIIa tomb and moved to Djer's tomb for safe keeping by an unknown thief. He bases this conjecture on one bracelet, found on the arm, that is decorated with *serekhs* on which falcons are perched. Citing stylistic studies, he proposes that this motif was no longer used by Djer's time and must have come from an earlier tomb. Apparently, although this point is not clear, other bracelets found on the mummified arm are the only close parallels for the bilobate beads from tomb L 24.[130] In contrast, W. M. F. Petrie dates the bracelet with *serekhs* and falcons to early in the reign of Djer.[131] The mummified arm was wrapped in linen, but no evidence exists to suggest that mummies were wrapped in linen during the Naqada IIIa period, as they were in the First Dynasty.[132] The bracelet consists of individual and alternating plaques of gold and turquoise. The earliest and closest parallels for these plaques are lapis lazuli and ivory plaques that were found in the same tomb.[133] The evidence, therefore, supports Petrie's dating for the bracelet. Finally, Williams's analysis shows that the iconography on the Qustul incense burner has parallels dating as early as the Naqada II period and as late as the First Dynasty.[134]

It therefore is clear that too many conflicting factors must be accommodated for tomb L 24 to fit the chronology that Williams has constructed for Cemetery L. If we consider instead the First Dynasty, the only real difficulty is that some of the pottery may be too early, but it is possible that these old pots were heirlooms that had some sentimental value to the occupant of the tomb. The importance of heirlooms and their collection is a human trait that seems to transcend cultural boundaries. The Egyptian ripple-flaked blade recovered from the previously mentioned Palestinian tomb is one example. At the southern Mesopotamian site of Uruk a beautifully carved vase dating to the Uruk period was recovered from a temple that is firmly dated to the Jamdat Nasr period. What is interesting about this vase is that it was saved in spite of having been badly broken.[135] The example that best illustrates this practice of collecting heirlooms comes from Egypt. Below the pyramid of Djoser, first king of the Third Dynasty, approximately 40,000 stone vessels were discovered dating to the First and Second Dynasties.[136] Therefore, the discovery of a few heirlooms from a grave in Nubia should not come as a surprise. Another theory proposed by W. Y. Adams is that since tomb robbing was a popular industry in ancient Egypt, it is possible that various stolen items from older tombs may have been passé and of little value in Upper Egypt, but they still could be used as trade goods in Nubia.[137] A similar situation occurs during the Eighteenth Dynasty when Egyptians exported goods pillaged from older Egyptian tombs to Crete.[138] According to the archaeological evidence from tomb L 24, then, it seems that the tomb should be dated to the early First Dynasty, as should the Qustul incense burner. Therefore, based on the evidence, the Nubian incense burners, the Scorpion macehead, and the Metropolitan Museum knife handle all date to the unification of Egypt or later. Furthermore, when we take into account that the earliest evidence of the White Crown appears on a Susan cylinder seal, and the earliest depiction of the White Crown in Egyptian iconography is in association with Mesopotamian-style high-ended ships, then it is feasible that the White Crown is a Mesopotamian import. This in turn would strengthen the possibility that the second register on the reverse of the Narmer palette depicts Narmer usurping the regalia of the northern king.

This theory is supported by some textual evidence that suggests a connection between the White Crown and Buto. Of all the gods, Osiris appears to be most closely associated with the White Crown. This association is so strong that by the Nineteenth Dynasty Osiris is described as wearing his crown as he leaves the womb.[139] Moreover, Osiris appears to either come from Mesopotamia or is an amalgamation of an Egyptian and Mesopotamian god. The earliest form of the name of Osiris consists of two ideograms, one of which denotes a "seat" and the other an "eye". Asar was the title of the Mesopotamian god Marduk, and his name is written with the same two ideograms. Osiris also appears to have strong ties to Byblos.[140]

The Pyramid Texts, which contain the earliest mention of Osiris were recovered from pyramids of the Fifth and Sixth Dynasties. Some of the texts, however, are believed to be much older and possibly based on oral tradition that dates to the Predynastic period. This span of time is reflected in the different burial customs mentioned, from predynastic sand graves to brick mastabas and finally to stone pyramids.[141]

These texts clearly indicate that by the Fifth Dynasty Osiris and the White Crown were associated with Upper Egypt and the Red Crown with Lower Egypt,[142] but earlier associations connecting Buto, Osiris, and the White Crown still survive in the Pyramid Texts. In these texts Osiris is identified with the dead king and his son Horus is identified with the living king. When Isis, the consort of Osiris, wails after finding Osiris dead, only the gods of Buto come to mourn.[143] Isis, who is the deified throne,[144] then gives birth to Horus while hiding at Khemmis, and Khemmis is an island that appears to be located in a marshy area in or near Pe (Buto),[145] and the word "Pe" in Egyptian also means seat or throne.[146] The birth of Horus at Buto is important because the eye of Horus is identified with the White Crown, and Horus gave this crown to his father Osiris.[147] Samuel Mercer explains this association between the White Crown and Horus by proposing that the Horus kings conquered the South before the time of Menes.[148]

Archaeological discoveries have disproved this early belief of a conquest of the South by Deltaic tribes, but a predynastic connection between Buto and the White Crown still remains and is supported by Pyramid Text § 455–456, which reads "take the Wrrt-[great White] crown from the great and mighty talkers [or foreigners](?)[149] who preside over Libya and from Sobk (Sebek), Lord of Baku."[150] As previously mentioned in this chapter, Libya or Tjehenu of predynastic times was probably located in the western Delta and included the Deltaic sites of Sais and Buto. The location of Baku is not as clear. Sobk is a crocodile god and, during dynastic times, the crocodile god was worshipped at Crocodilopolis in the Fayum. According to A. H. Gardiner, a number of deities were identified with the western Delta during predynastic times, and Sobk is the son of the goddess Neith of Sais, who is also known as Neith of Tjehenu.[151] During the Sed Festival, the crocodile-god Sobk is associated with the sites of Pe and Dep (Buto).[152] It has been proposed recently that the crocodile god of the dynastic times may have been a Lower Egyptian king during the Predynastic period. It is possible then that Sobk may have originally been a Lower Egyptian king who was later deified.[153]

Baku also appears to have been associated with Tjehenu and was probably located somewhere in the western Delta.[154] Therefore, based on the previous evidence, if Libya or Tjehenu did include the western part of the Delta during the Predynastic period as previously discussed, then this passage may be alluding to the wresting of the White Crown from foreigners who ruled or had influence over this region. This passage supports the proposition that the White Crown had an early connection with the Delta, and the possibility that the White Crown is a foreign import, possibly from Susa, also, gains some support from this passage.

Besides the White Crown, Narmer also wears a belt and a tail. Four Hathor heads hang from this belt, and, as previously mentioned, Hathor is associated with Buto. The tail is not only worn by Egyptians, but it is commonly associated with the people of Tjehenu.[155] The belt and tail may also be part of the clothing stripped from the former ruler.

Behind Narmer is his sandal- or cylinder-seal bear, who is associated with the rosette. As Baumgartel previously pointed out, the rosette has its closest parallels from Mesopotamia, but its meaning is unknown. During this period of unification, the rosette is found on the Narmer palette and macehead, the Scorpion macehead, and the Metropolitan Museum handle, and the iconography on each of these artifacts depicts events that appear to take place in the Delta. After the unification, the rosette is never again displayed in such a prominent context. It may therefore have had a special meaning in Lower Egyptian iconography.

In front of Narmer is the falcon-god Horus, which signifies Narmer. In early times Horus, when representing the Delta, was known as "Horus of Libya who lifts his arm"[156] and "Horus of Tjehenu, high of arm."[157] These titles seem to be an appropriate description of this engraving of Horus rendered on the Narmer palette, who, with arm held high, is grasping a rope by which he brings prisoners from the Delta. Kneeling before Narmer is the vanquished Chief of the Harpoon nome; this chief may have had his capital at Buto. A Lower Egyptian kingdom of Buto is alluded to in the Pyramid Texts.[158]

If this interpretation is correct, then the second register on the Narmer palette portrays Narmer stripping the King of Buto of his regalia and at the same time humiliating him to exhibit his impotence before the might of the new king. One of the difficulties in evaluating this royal regalia is that we have a tendency to associate it primarily with a geographical location. But the regalia, especially the White Crown, also have a religious meaning that transcends geographic boundaries. Osiris, wearer of the White Crown, is identified with the dead king, while Horus is identified with the living king. Being identified with Horus establishes a connection with the legitimate

line. The king rules essentially as heir of all previous kings.[159] Frankfort points out that the ancient Egyptians believed that objects are
endowed with power.[160] Therefore, Narmer's stripping the former
king of his regalia, especially if it includes the White Crown, is important in that the power inherent in the White Crown establishes
legitimacy between Narmer and the previous kings of Lower Egypt.
A possible vestige of this early connection is seen during the corona-
tion of Queen Hatshepsut when she is described as "daughter of the
white crown, beloved of Buto."[161]

With respect to the third register, there appears to be only one
point on which everyone agrees: the sign above the prostrate man on
the left is a fortress, even though we have no evidence that any fortress resembling this sign existed so early. If, however, we compare
this sign to an outline of Neith-hotep's tomb or a Mesopotamian
temple, we see a strong resemblance (figs. 28, 29, and 50). The Deltaic town closest to the royal cemetery, or a town renowned for its
Mesopotamian-style temple or palace, may thus be represented. If
this interpretation is correct, the three *inb* signs on a First Dynasty
seal may signify Memphis and indicate that, at one time, Mesopotamian-style temples or palaces stood in the town. An alternative interpretation is that the *inb* sign originally meant a crenelated tomb, in
which case, the seal displays the elements of a cemetery, with the
three *inb* signs representing tombs and the other building signs, funerary temples. This second interpretation would explain why the
inb sign was bestowed upon Memphis. It was the town associated
with the cemetery of Saqqara, where most of the tombs with crenelated facades were built during the First Dynasty. The sign may have
designated first the cemetery and later Memphis. This is in fact how
Memphis acquired its name, which originally belonged to the pyramid of Phiops I of the Sixth Dynasty: only later was it given to the
city.[162] Considering that cones used to decorate such buildings were
found at Buto, that Buto may have been the center of a kingdom
during the Predynastic period, and that the souls of dead kings are
believed to reside at Buto,[163] it is possible that this sign was first used
to designate Buto because it was the site closest to the cemetery. Also,
the earliest description of the prototype of a royal funerary burial in
the Delta is found in Pyramid Text § 179–193. The place names included suggest this type of burial comes from the northwest Delta
region, and one of the sites named was Dep (Buto).[164] This scenario
is reflected in a translation of Pyramid Text § 561–562 by Frankfort.

He states that "our text [suggests] that King Teti, because he is buried at Pe (Buto), survives the crises of death."[165]

The sign to the right of the *inb* sign in the third register may represent Sais. It should also be noted that this sign is similar to a design used to decorate buildings with crenelated facades in Mesopotamia,[166] suggesting that this design was borrowed from Mesopotamia. According to J. Leibovitch, this sign is an early representation of a "double lotus" motif.[167] The double lotus motif is commonly seen as a decorative motif on crenelated funerary structures engraved on funerary stelae; such stelae appear to be most commonly recovered from mastabas at Giza in Lower Egypt that date to the Old Kingdom.[168] It is possible, therefore, that both the crenelated building sign and this "double lotus" motif were important aspects of predynastic tombs in Lower Egypt, and both signs together are meant to represent the Lower Egyptian site that was closest to the royal cemetery, possibly another name for Buto.

As previously mentioned, the two prostrate men may be Asiatic, and I will reiterate Smith's premise that the Delta had a diverse ethnic population during the Predynastic period.[169] If some Deltaic towns had assimilated Mesopotamian architectural features, such as crenelated facades and clay cones, then it is also possible that they may have copied some personal characteristics, such as long hair and beards, which were used to describe foreigners during the First Dynasty. One of the earliest depictions of a foreigner in Egypt is of a Mesopotamian carved on the handle of the Gebel el Arak knife (fig. 40).

The second register on the obverse of the Narmer palette shows Narmer, wearing the Red Crown, with his entourage. The procession may be starting from a building, such as a temple, and is proceeding through "The Great Door" of Buto to inspect the decapitated bodies of his enemy (fig. 49).

The large felines with entwined serpent necks are depicted in the third register. As previously mentioned, a number of symbolic interpretations have been attributed to this motif. Unfortunately, it is difficult if not impossible to ascertain the validity of these interpretations. It could be that this motif was copied from a cylinder seal like the one believed to be from northern Syria (figs. 49, 55), and was chosen only because the ability to restrain two mythical animals is a visually powerful motif that enhances the power of the king and effectively symbolizes the subjugation of the north.

It has been argued that all predynastic motifs from Susa or Mesopotamia cease to enter Egypt at the end of the Naqada II period. Therefore, the Mesopotamian motifs we see on late predynastic artifacts such as the Narmer palette are all Egyptianized versions of earlier Mesopotamian motifs.[170] This view is undoubtably correct in regard to some motifs like the long-necked felines on the obverse of the Smaller palette of Hierakonpolis. The only similarities between these two felines with Mesopotamian examples is the retention of their long necks. In contrast, the felines on the Narmer palette have changed little from those depicted on the Syrian cylinder seal. It seems unlikely that a motif would remain static for so long when similar motifs changed so radically during the same time.

The belief that the feline motif on the Narmer palette is Egyptianized is also placed in doubt when we consider the evolution of this motif in Mesopotamia. Originally, this motif was a combination of the intertwined snakes (fig. 19) attached to the bodies of two lions. On the earliest Mesopotamian examples the snake heads are retained. The snake heads are then replaced by lion heads and eventually the necks are shortened.[171] The motif portrayed on the Syrian cylinder seal is one of the latest versions of this motif, and the feline motif on the Narmer palette is the latest Egyptian example until the Middle Kingdom. For this to be a coincidence is unlikely. Instead, this motif probably bears such a strong resemblance to the one on the cylinder seal because it was copied from an item that had recently been imported into Egypt. This motif is important because it suggests that Buto had contact with sites with strong Mesopotamian ties until its fall at the beginning of the First Dynasty. This would explain why this motif and others that appear to have been copied from Mesopotamian imports quickly disappear after the time of the Narmer palette. The adoption of griffins, long-necked felines, and rosettes may be an indication that a port city like Buto would have been more accepting of outside influences than a relatively homogenous culture situated in an environment shielded from other cultures, as seen in Upper Egypt. Only aspects of Lower Egyptian culture that were firmly ingrained would have survived after Buto fell to the south. In contrast, the succeeding dynastic culture would have been resistant to outside influences and would have carried on trade for textiles, oils, and raw materials.

Finally, in the fourth register the ka-like structure could represent Sais or Buto before its fall to Narmer. The sites of Buto and Sais are continually mentioned throughout this review. Thus, the final subjugation of the Delta may have been realized by the conquest of these two sites. Or this palette may have been carved to depict the fall of Buto, the last and most important of the Lower Egyptian sites.

The Mesopotamian signs and motifs on the Narmer palette become much more understandable if we accept the possibility that the Delta was the entrepôt for Mesopotamian goods during the Naqada II and III periods. If this interpretation of the Mesopotamian elements on the palette is valid, it then follows that northern Mesopotamia continued to have a strong influence on Lower Egypt at least as late as the unification. The relevance of this sustained influence will be clarified in the next chapter.

11 TRADE ROUTES

A review of possible trade goods and their distribution clearly shows that northern Mesopotamia was a center for trade that connected Egypt, Susa, and southern Mesopotamia. It also seems to indicate that more than one trade route linked Egypt with northern Mesopotamia and that routes and trade centers changed through time.

According to the archaeological evidence presented in this study, it appears that northern Mesopotamia went through three phases of trade activity that extend from late in the Ubaid period to at least the early part of the Jamdat Nasr period.

Small villages like Tepe Gawra appear to have benefited most during the first phase, which opens with the appearance there of stamp seals and numerous trade items, such as gold and lapis lazuli, in level XIII. Gold, lapis lazuli, and other trade goods increased in volume, especially in level X. Tepe Gawra's trade ties were extensive. They included Sialk to the east, the Amuq region to the west, Norşun-tepe in Anatolia, southern Mesopotamia to the south, and possibly even Palestine and Egypt. The precise nature of Tepe Gawra's trade ties, whether direct or indirect, is not clear. The appearance of lapis lazuli beads in Palestine at about the same time that lapis lazuli appears in Egypt and that gold becomes abundant at Tepe Gawra suggests that Egypt and Tepe Gawra may have been trading via Palestine. It is also possible that this lapis lazuli was acquired from Egypt, but, even so, there appears to be little doubt that Palestinian sites were participating in at least indirect trade with Syria. The appearance of silver at Byblos during the "énéolithique" period, and of triangular-lugged pottery, tubular-spouted pottery, and multiple-brush painting in Egypt during the Naqada IIa period (and possibly

faience as early as the Naqada I period), all suggest a second route by
sea between Egypt and northern Syria.

Unfortunately, little is known about prehistoric seafaring from
northern Syria, along the Syro-Palestinian coast, to Egypt. According to G. F. Bass, "long before there were shepherds or farmers in
Greece there were sailors."[1] It appears as if the same can be said for
the entire Levant, because we now know that early hunters sailed to
Cyprus around 8500 B.C.[2] Fishing and sea trade were probably the
basis for the establishment of sites such as Byblos and Ras Shamra.
Considering that millennia separate these early seafarers from the
end of the Ubaid period, a network of maritime trade routes could
easily have developed throughout the Levant.

In regard to a land route, the most likely passage connecting
Tepe Gawra to Egypt via Palestine would seem to be through northern Syria to the Amuq region and then south through Hama to Palestine; archaeological evidence suggests that a trade route connecting
Anatolia and Palestine passed through Hama during the Ubaid period, and, at the same time, this site also reflects Mesopotamian influences. Mesopotamian influence continues to be felt at Hama during
the Uruk period, but this appears to be a period of diminishing trade
on this route,[3] which coincides with the beginning of a long occupational hiatus at Ras Shamra. No direct evidence exists to indicate
what land route replaced this north-south route through Hama, but
one may have extended through the Transjordan Desert and culmi-
nated with the foundation of a site at Jawa during the next phase of
trade activity.

The second phase commences with the appearance of Mesopotamian "colonies" in northern Mesopotamia. There are two types of
Mesopotamian sites during this phase: "colonies" like Habuba Kabira that had no agricultural base and survived solely on trade, and
northern Mesopotamian sites like Tell Brak that enjoyed an agricultural base, but that were influenced to some extent by southern Mesopotamia. This second phase appears to coincide with the Late Uruk
period to the south[4] and at least Gawra IX to the north.[5]

The appearance of Uruk sites and Uruk influence at indigenous
sites in northern Mesopotamia seems to be a result of increased de-
mand for raw materials in southern Mesopotamia and a desire to tap
into the growing east-west trade that was so obviously profitable in
the villages to the north as seen with Tepe Gawra. The appearance
of these sites may also be owing to the inability of indigenous com-

munities in northern Mesopotamia to acquire, process, and transport the increasing amounts of raw materials and trade goods that growing populations like southern Mesopotamia and Egypt required. Weiss states that "because copper, when available through long-distance trade, perhaps with Anatolia and Iran, was apparently very costly, baked-clay sickles and even axes were often used in place of copper tools."[6] It is possible that this situation had less to do with the cost of copper than with the inability of early traders to procure and transport enough copper to satisfy the needs of the people of southern Mesopotamia.

The voluminous trade through northern Mesopotamia is best illustrated by the fact that a complex the size of Habuba Kabira, with a population of 6,000 to 8,000 inhabitants, could be built and then maintained for a period of 100 to 150 years while the city's population, instead of growing their own food, acquires it from the indigenous population.[7] Such a community was clearly dependent for its survival on a large annual trade volume. Survival was even more difficult if the colonies were founded by competing southern Mesopotamian communities in the manner of colonies founded by the Greeks in the eighth century B.C.[8] This would suggest that a large number of colonies were competing for a limited number of resources. The colonies in northern Mesopotamia evidently had a major impact on Tepe Gawra, which by level IX had changed from a relatively large, secular, trading town to a small religious center.[9] Thus, the center of trade in the north seems to have shifted from Tepe Gawra to the colonies during this second phase.

The chronological correlations among the colonies, Egypt, and Palestine appear reliable because, as previously noted, late Uruk pottery, cylinder seals, and motifs are found primarily during the Naqada IIc/d period in Egypt, and what appear to be the remains of a Palestinian ledge-handle jar of late chalcolithic date and a piece of Nubian ware of Naqada IIc date have been found at Habuba Kabira.

Again, the large, fortified site of Jawa in the Transjordan Desert may have been a transshipment point between northern Syria and Palestine during this second phase, as it was during the Middle Bronze Age. Jawa, like the Mesopotamian colonies, appeared suddenly, existed for a short period, and then was abandoned. The pottery, fortifications, and water management systems reflect influences from both Palestine and Syria.[10] Pottery from Jawa and Habuba Kabira suggest that these sites are contemporary. Thus Jawa, like Habuba

Kabira, may have been built in order to access and increase the trade between northern Mesopotamia and Palestine in this second phase.

The distribution patterns of pottery, raw materials, cylinder seals, and motifs indicate that a second route through northern Syria and then by sea to Egypt continued in use and was greatly expanded with the appearance of the colonies in northern Syria. Although goods probably traveled to Palestine and then possibly to Egypt via Jawa, a direct sea route would have carried the bulk of the trade. The large volume of cargo that a few small ships can carry is not fully appreciated by most scholars. The Late Bronze Age shipwreck at Uluburun will illustrate the point.

The bulk of the cargo that was being carried by this ship consisted of such commodities as copper, tin, glass ingots, elephant and hippopotamus ivory, ebony logs, murex opercula, ostrich eggshells, tortoise carapaces, seashell rings,[11] orpiment or yellow arsenic, terebinth resin,[12] figs (or fig products),[13] scrap-gold jewelry,[14] large quantities of beads made from agate, amber, faience, glass, and ostrich eggshell,[15] as well as pomegranates, coriander, grapes, olives (possibly olive oil and wine), nuts (almond and pine),[16] and cedar.[17] If this ship had made its destination, most, if not all of these goods would have disappeared from the archaeological record as they were consumed or transformed into finished products.

This wreck highlights not only the variety of invisible trade goods aboard this one ship but also the large quantities of such goods. If we were to collect all the bronze from all known Late Bronze Age land sites, we would probably have only a fraction of the amount of tin and copper recovered from this one shipwreck (ca. 11 tons), and the copper and tin from this one shipwreck represent only a small fraction of what was produced, traded, and shipped in the Late Bronze Age. Therefore because a few small ships could transport relatively large quantities of goods between Egypt and northern Syria every year from the Late Predynastic period through the beginning of the First Dynasty, great quantities of raw materials and unfinished goods could have been exchanged between such distant sites as Egypt and northern Mesopotamia without leaving much trace in the archaeological record.

We know that the Naqada IIc period coincides with the disappearance of the Maadi culture in most of Lower Egypt, the establishment of Naqada II sites in the eastern Delta, an increase in Upper Egyptian influence in the northern Sinai, and a corresponding in crease of influence at Ain Besor, Tel Erani, and Azor in Palestine. This Upper Egyptian expansion into Palestine is believed to have been the result of increasing trade between Lower Egypt and Palestine and possibly a need for copper in Egypt. Another reason for expansion into Palestine may have been to control trade with northern Syria. A similar situation is seen in northern Syria with the appearance of the southern Mesopotamian colonies.

In classical times, according to Lionel Casson, a ship with favorable winds could make roughly 4.5 to 6 knots. The best that could be expected for a day's sail would be about 185 kilometers.[18] Unfortunately, we know little about the rigging and construction of ships during the Predynastic period, but it is safe to accept that the best sailing times were less than 185 kilometers per day. The distance from the eastern Delta to southern Palestine is approximately 200 kilometers, and to Byblos it is approximately 450 to 500 kilometers, depending on whether a ship sails directly to Byblos or hugs the coast.[19] Clearly, if the Upper Egyptians were able to gain control of the eastern Delta and the northern Sinai, and extend their influence to sites like Ain Besor, Tell Erani, and Azor in southern Palestine, they could make sea trade between Buto and the Levant very difficult and exploit trade through Jawa. They would also be in a position to wrest control of the sea route from Byblos (fig. 7). This would explain why the disappearance of silver from Byblos coincides with the appearance of the same type of silver at Azor and with an increase in Egyptian influence in Palestine and Lower Egypt. As previously mentioned, it is during the Naqada IIc/d period that the earliest Mesopotamian imports, Susan motifs, and an abundance of lapis lazuli appear in Upper Egypt. Since this coincides with an Upper Egyptian expansion into Lower Egypt and the eastern Delta, it is perhaps an indication that the Naqada II people were attempting to tap into or take control of the sea and land routes between Buto and northern Syria.

At the same time that trade between Egypt and northern Mesopotamia commenced, an occupational hiatus began at Ras Shamra.[20] Perhaps goods were brought to Byblos from northern Mesopotamia by land and were then shipped to Egypt. Such a land route would have bypassed Ras Shamra, possibly pressuring the populace into relocating. If this is what happened, we would expect to find evidence of strong Mesopotamian influence at Byblos, but there is little.[21] Further, Hama would have been on the land route to Byblos, but, as noted earlier, this route seems to have diminished in importance by this time. Instead, it appears that primarily Anatolia and Egypt were influencing Byblos, which suggests that Byblos was a transshipment point between the two areas. Ras Shamra is located approximately 160 kilometers (by direct sailing) to 200 kilometers (by hugging the coast) north of Byblos. It is also approximately 50 kilometers south of the mouth of the Orontes River, which passes near Tell Judeidah. If Mesopotamian goods were coming to the sea via Tell Judeidah, then Ras Shamra would have been in a good position to take advantage of the trade, but since Ras Shamra was abandoned and Tell Judeidah was not heavily influenced by the Mesopotamian colonies, it seems unlikely that this was the main route. Another possibility is that goods were being shipped from the Bay of Iskanderia approximately 190 kilometers north of Ras Shamra, which lay too far south to control activity in the bay. If goods were being shipped from the Bay of Iskanderia to Byblos, then Ras Shamra would have suffered from a poor location that would have transformed it from a major entrepôt to a backwater in a short time.

The second trade phase ends with the disappearance of the Mesopotamian colonies, which is usually considered to be the result of a major collapse to the south that signaled a reorganization of southern Mesopotamian society. This situation may be more intricate than previously thought. In view of the size of Habuba Kabira, its reliance on the local population for agricultural goods, and strong competition with surrounding sites for trade, it is possible that this type of community was doomed to failure at its inception. Any disruption in trade for even a short time could have forced the abandonment of these settlements. For example, fighting between Upper and Lower Egypt during the Naqada IId or the Naqada III periods could easily have disrupted trade between Egypt and northern Mesopotamia for a number of years, and, if this disruption coincided with an increasing availability of copper from Oman, and other raw materials from Iran, such settlements could be forced into oblivion rather rapidly. I am not proposing that a war in Egypt was the cause of the disappearance of the colonies, but that a disruption in the trade of either copper from Anatolia, gold from Egypt, or lapis lazuli from the East for even a relatively short period could have led to such a disappearance, and to unrest for any other participants in this trade network.

Finally, according to C. C. Lamberg-Karlovsky, it is possible that the establishment of the colonies may have been legitimized by religious ideology, which may have been a driving force for expansion during the Late Uruk period.[22] This impetus may also have led to unrealistic expectations manifest in the establishment of too many colonies that were too large to survive.

The third trade phase is dominated by northern Mesopotamian sites, such as Tell Brak, with southern Mesopotamian influence. The disappearance of the colonies, instead of reflecting a collapse of Uruk influence in northern Mesopotamia, may be an indication of a population shift to more stable sites like Tell Brak that allowed trade to continue in a more efficient manner. This realignment would have led to the increased wealth at Tell Brak evidenced by the construction of the Grey Eye Temple.

This third phase seems to coincide with at least the Naqada IIIb period through the beginning of the First Dynasty in Egypt. The appearance of Mesopotamian motifs on the Narmer palette, monkey figurines and decorated maceheads at Tell Brak, the continued appearance of lapis lazuli in Egypt until the end of Djer's reign and at Tell Brak during the beginning of Jamdat Nasr period may indicate that trade between Egypt and northern Mesopotamia did not stop at the end of the Naqada II period but continued until the end of Djer's reign. Such trade would have depended mainly upon a direct sea route between Egypt and northern Syria.

Helene Kantor continues to have reservations concerning a sea route connecting Egypt with northern Syria because of the lack of Mesopotamian artifacts and influence at Byblos and sites in Palestine.[23] We continue to have this rather romantic image of early seafarers hugging the coasts as they sail in their small ships because of their fear of the sea. Such an image may be inaccurate. As previously mentioned, voyages were made to Cyprus as early as 8500 B.C. A considerable amount can be learned in sailing these waters for five millennia. It is possible that trade was carried on at different levels. Local and regional trade, which was performed by individuals, probably consisted of frequent stops at seaside villages during a voyage. Luxury goods from greater distances may have been carried in ships owned by towns or small kingdoms. A voyage from Egypt to northern Syria would take best advantage of the prevailing currents by sailing up the coasts of Palestine, Lebanon, and Syria. A return voyage following the same route would be more difficult because a ship must sail against the currents. Instead, a ship could make a much quicker voyage by sailing due west from the Bay of Iskanderia along the southern coast of Turkey; after passing Cyprus, the North and Northwest winds and southeastern currents would result in a fast passage to Egypt. Such a route would give western Deltaic sites like Buto a definite trade advantage with northern Syria. Under these conditions, we would not expect to find Mesopotamian goods at sites like Byblos because ships stopping to trade and resupply, regardless of their origin, would be carrying mainly Egyptian goods.

The argument for direct trade with Egypt via southern Mesopotamia has been based largely upon the distribution of Mesopotamian artifacts in southern Egypt, and the appearance of "foreign" vessels with high ends on the Gebel el Arak knife, the Hierakonpolis mural, and rock paintings in the Wadi Hammamat. A study of these high-ended ships has shown that the vessels on the Hierakonpolis mural and the rock paintings may have evolved from a similar vessel that is portrayed on a Naqada I sherd. If the high ends depicted on these paintings are attributable to Mesopotamian influences, it is obvious that they, like the master of animals on the Hierakonpolis mural, have been assimilated by Upper Egyptian culture and are not evidence of direct contact. There is little doubt that the high-ended vessels and the master of animals on the Gebel el Arak knife are the product of close contact with Mesopotamia. A study of the motifs on this knife handle suggests that it was carved in the Delta and could have been taken to the south as a result of trade or conquest.

The distribution pattern of Mesopotamian artifacts in southern Egypt is the strongest argument for direct trade with southern Mesopotamia, but Mesopotamian artifacts and artifacts bearing Mesopotamian motifs are rare in Upper Egypt, especially when considering the length of the period under study. Most of these artifacts were also found in association with lapis lazuli, which seems to suggest that both came to Egypt via the same route. Moreover, because the appearance of these materials is contemporary with the expansion of Upper Egyptian culture into northern Egypt and southern Palestine and the appearance of Mesopotamian and Susan colonies in northern Syria and Iran, the distribution pattern of these artifacts supports the use of a northern trade route.

The evidence for southern Mesopotamian trade around the Persian Gulf is also clear. By the Jamdat Nasr period in southern Mesopotamia, trade was thriving with the Iranian cities to the east, and southern Mesopotamia appears to have begun importing copper from Oman via Dilmun. By the beginning of the Early Dynastic period, the evidence increases significantly for trade between southern Mesopotamia and Dilmun. Spouted or collared containers with direct parallels to those at Uruk become common in Bahrain. Carved chlorite and steatite bowls with strong affinities to Mesopotamian containers are also abundant in this area. In Oman, buff-ware and painted jars with parallels to Mesopotamian jars are found. The appearance of faience beads and of plano-convex bricks may also be a result of contacts between Mesopotamia and Oman.

The evidence for an expansion of trade between Mesopotamia and Dilmun is also reflected in the texts. By early dynastic times the name Dilmun becomes quite common,[24] and both the archaeological and textual evidence suggest a continual growth of trade between southern Mesopotamia and Dilmun from the end of the Uruk period through the Early Dynastic period. In contrast, we lack evidence suggesting that southern Mesopotamia was participating in direct trade outside the Persian Gulf. In regard to Egypt, we not only lack evidence for a direct route on which sailing ships carried cargoes between Egypt and southern Mesopotamia at this early period, but we lack evidence for such a route throughout antiquity and modern times.

In Egypt, the First Dynasty was a period of experimentation, cultural development, expansion, and growth.[25] This growth is evident in the area of trade. Large quantities of imported vessels from Syria and Palestine, presumably for oils and perfumes, are commonly found in both royal and private tombs.[26] This acquisition of large quantities of foreign oils and perfumes and possibly textiles appears to be common as early as the Naqada IIIa period, during the reign of the ruler who was interred in tomb U-j at Abydos. Also during the First Dynasty, at some southern sites in Palestine, such as Tel Erani, Egyptian pottery is so abundant that it is believed that Egyptians lived on the site.[27] The archaeological evidence also suggests that trade between Egypt and the East intensified during this period. Therefore, because trade in the Persian Gulf continued to expand from the Jamdat Nasr period through early dynastic times, and because Egypt's trade relations with Syria and Palestine intensified during the same period, we would expect trade between Egypt and Mesopotamia to increase. Yet, Mesopotamian influences disappear from Egypt during the First Dynasty. If a southern route around Arabia connected these two cultures, this sudden absence of ties is at present inexplicable. Instead, the evidence strongly suggests that trade between Egypt and northern Syria continues to grow as late as the First Dynasty. What appears to change is that the Egyptians had little interest in motifs and finished goods from the north and were mainly interested in more basic items such as raw materials and oils. Therefore, the archaeological evidence for trade patterns during the Predynastic period and into the First Dynasty suggests that most trade between Egypt and Mesopotamia was carried out via northern Syria and the Mediterranean Sea as a result of an expansion of previously established trade routes in these regions.

NOTES

CHAPTER 1. INTRODUCTION

1. Bénédite 1916; Petrie 1917; Rostovtzeff 1920; Langdon 1921; Hall 1922.
2. Frankfort 1924, 93–143; Frankfort 1941.
3. Kantor 1942; 1944, 111–31; 1949; 1952; 1965, 11–14; 1992, 1:11–17.
4. Baumgartel 1955, 44–50; Ward 1964, 3–5, 11–29.
5. Bissing 1929, 75–76; 1943, 481–516; Kelly 1974.
6. Ward 1964, 33–36; Helck 1971, 6–9.
7. Frankfort 1924, 140, 142; Kantor 1965, 11–14; Baumgartel 1955, 44–50.
8. Forbes 1965a, 2:196–206.
9. Winkler 1938, 18–41.
10. Kantor 1965, 13.
11. Ward 1964, 34.

CHAPTER 2. HISTORY AND TRADE OF EARLY MESOPOTAMIA

1. Porada 1965, 142–44, 149–52; Mallowan 1980, 330–53, 357–59, 376–83, 388–98. Unless noted otherwise, all dates for Levantine and Mesopotamian sites will be based on Schwartz and Weiss 1992, 1:221–36.
2. Watson 1965, 69–73; Mallowan 1980, 413–20.
3. Moorey 1982, 14.
4. Oates 1993, 409.
5. Potts 1990, 41–47, 50–61.
6. Roaf and Galbraith 1994, 770–78.
7. Oates 1983, 256.
8. Potts 1990, 20–21.
9. Oates 1983, 256.
10. Rice 1991, 65.

11. Potts 1990, 21, 69–70, 80–81.

12. Harlan 1992, 60.

13. Rowley-Conwy 1991, 205–209.

14. Porada 1965, 145–49; Mallowan 1980, 388–97.

15. Porada 1965, 153–56; Mallowan 1980, 355–57, 360–64; Frankfort and Davies 1980, 74–81.

16. Crawford 1973, 232–39.

17. Tell Qannas appears to have been the administrative center of Habuba Kabira, and Jebel Aruda is 8 kilometers upstream from Habuba Kabira. Owing to the close proximity of these three sites, Habuba Kabira will designate them on all maps in this study.

18. Moorey 1982, 14–15; Potts 1990, 91–92.

19. Yakar 1984, 65–67.

20. Moorey 1982, 15; Potts 1990, 63–64, 72–76, 86–92.

21. Potts 1990, 85–86.

22. Ibid., 63–64, 72–76, 85–92.

CHAPTER 3. HISTORY AND TRADE OF PREDYNASTIC EGYPT

1. The Predynastic chronology of Upper Egyptian sites is based on Hoffman 1988, 33–46. At the present some argue that the early phase of the Badarian period should be classified as a separate Tasian period. I have decided to use a standard chronology because the Tasian period is not pertinent to the issues raised in this study. For those interested in this problem, see Brunton 1937, 25–33; Baumgartel 1974, 468; Kantor 1965, 4; Kantor 1992, 1:7–8.

2. Brunton and Caton-Thompson 1928, 5–42; Hayes 1965, 147; Hoffman 1991, 136–43.

3. Brunton and Caton-Thompson 1928, 41.

4. Kantor 1992, 1:12.

5. Brunton and Caton-Thompson 1928, 24.

6. Hoffman 1991, 16.

7. Hayes 1965, 94.

8. Caton-Thompson and Gardner 1934, 35; Banks 1980.

9. Caton-Thompson and Gardner 1934, 34, 41–43; Hassan 1984, 60.

10. Brewer 1989, 28, 109–19.

11. Caton-Thompson and Gardner 1934, 34, 72, 84, 87–88, 90. See also, Eiwanger 1984, n. 252.

12. Hayes 1965, 93–99; Hoffman 1991, 185–86. For more information on recent surveys to the Fayum area refer to Casini 1984; Wenke 1984, 193–98; Dagnan-Ginter et al. 1984, 33–65, 93–99.

13. Hayes 1965, 92–93; Hoffman 1991, 16; Hawass, Hassan, and Gautier 1988, 31–38.

14. Junker 1929, 180–84; Hoffman 1991, 170, 173–81. See also, Caton-Thompson and Gardner 1934, 29, 32–34, 39, 45, 48, 70, 72, 78, 87, 89–94; Eiwanger 1988, 36–37.
15. Stern 1993, 1529.
16. Levy 1986, 96; Mazar 1990, 72.
17. Bar-Adon 1980, 243; Ilan and Sebbane 1989, 143; Gonen 1992, 60, 62, 67; see also Hanbury-Tenison 1986, 157–59.
18. Gonen 1992, 62; see also Reese, Mienis, and Woodward 1986, 79–80.
19. Hayes 1965, 109; Elliot 1978, 38; Gonen 1992, 58.
20. Kantor 1942, 175–76, 203; Kaplan 1959, 134; Hayes 1965, 106–107.
21. Kantor 1942, 175–76, 203; Kantor 1965, 6–7; Kaplan 1959, 134–36.
22. Elliot 1977, 3; Gonen 1992, 73.
23. Elliot 1977, 42.
24. Ibid., 44; Gonen 1992, 60.
25. Gonen 1992, 72.
26. Tobler 1950, 203–204; Hayes 1965, 109; Gonen 1992, 58.
27. Hayes 1965, 147–48; Williams 1980, 13; Adams 1985; Williams 1987, 15–26.
28. Smith 1991, 108.
29. Baumgartel 1974, 473–77; Hoffman 1984, 243; Krzyżaniak 1977, 101–23.
30. Rizkana and Seeher 1987, 76.
31. Petrie 1915, 42; Kaczmarczyk and Hedges 1983, A71–A78; Moorey 1985, 137.
32. Rizkana and Seeher 1987, 64–66. Disagreement exists as to the chronological placement of the Omari A group. See also, Debono and Mortensen 1990, 80–81.
33. Hayes 1965, 117–22; Debono and Mortensen 1990, 79–80.
34. Rizkana and Seeher 1989, 80–85.
35. Rizkana and Seeher 1987, 58–63, 66–80; Rizkana and Seeher 1989, 74–80, 83–85.
36. Hoffman 1991, 121, 152–53; Krzyżaniak 1977, 139–57.
37. Rizkana and Seeher 1987, 79–80; Rizkana and Seeher 1989, 83–85.
38. Way 1992, 3–5.
39. Oren 1989, 393, 400.
40. This presence is reflected by strata VIII–VI at Tel Erani. See Weinstein 1984, 63–64; Brandl 1989, 365, 372, 374.
41. This presence is reflected by stratum V at Tel Erani. See Weinstein 1984, 63–64; Brandl 1989, 365.
42. Ward 1991, 14.
43. Ben-Tor 1975, 26–30.
44. Ben-Tor 1986, 14.
45. Kantor 1965, 9–11.

46. Smith 1991, 108.
47. Hoffman 1988, 49–50.
48. Ibid., 44–45. In regard to the royal cemetery at Abydos see, Dreyer with Hartung and Pumpenmeier 1993.
49. Dreyer 1992, 295–99; Dreyer with Hartung and Pumpenmeier 1993, 34–35, 37.

CHAPTER 4. THE POTTERY

1. Kantor 1942, 182–84, 188–94; Ward 1964, 6–8; Kantor 1992, 1:13–14.
2. Perkins 1963, 80, 107; Lapp 1970, 118; Dunand 1973, fig. 164; Rizkana and Seeher 1987, 70, 72.
3. Ward 1964, 6, 8.
4. Ibid., 8; Hennessy 1967, 38.
5. Hennessy 1967, 38.
6. Ibid., 28, 38; Kantor 1992, 1:13.
7. Goldman 1956, 85, 90, and figs. 22, 232; Hennessy 1967, 28, 38.
8. See respectively Brunton 1937, 76; Petrie 1901a, pl. xix, 70; Brunton and Caton-Thompson 1928, 44. See also Baumgartel 1955, 94–95.
9. Kantor 1942, 176–77; Baumgartel 1955, 94–95.
10. See respectively, Starr 1937, 14; Mecquenem 1928, 103 and fig. 2; see also Baumgartel 1955, 95.
11. Perkins 1963, 99–108, 163, 166–67, 169, 195.
12. Kantor 1942, 188–89.
13. Kantor 1965, 8; Hennessy 1967, 30–31, 39.
14. Sürenhagen 1977, 60–88, and pls. 4–5, 9, 12, 14, 17; Algaze 1986b, 281.
15. Kantor 1965, 8; 1992, 1:14.
16. Kantor 1965, 10; Sürenhagen 1977, pls. 6–11, 18–19.
17. Kantor 1992, 1:14.
18. Algaze 1986, 281.
19. Petrie 1915, 18, and pls. 31–35.
20. Braidwood 1939, 193–94; see also Thuesen 1988, 182.
21. Sürenhagen 1986, 22.
22. Way 1987, 247, and figs. 3.1–4.
23. Schwartz and Weiss 1992, 1:232–33.
24. The following citation supports all prior statements in this paragraph. Potts 1990, 63–64, 72–76. For other possible parallels compare Petrie 1915, pls. 14.98, 16.32, and 16.34b, with Sürenhagen 1977, tabs. 13.85, 12.77, and 14.86.

CHAPTER 5. RAW MATERIALS

1. Lucas and Harris 1962, 52–63, 199–205, 224, 247–48, 391–95, 406–21.
2. Ibid., 199–205.
3. Hoffman 1991, 207–208; Rizkana and Seeher 1989, 78–79; Ward 1991, 16–17.
4. Nibbi 1985, 13–14; Lucas and Harris 1962, 429–48; see also Ben-Tor 1991, 4; Ward 1991, 13–14.
5. Butzer 1976, 13.
6. Schmidt 1992, 34.
7. Zarins 1989, 340–42, 355–68.
8. Lucas 1928; Lucas and Harris 1962, 234–35, 245–47, 491; Gale and Stos-Gale 1981, 103, 109.
9. Moorey 1985, 108; Gale and Stos-Gale 1981, 107.
10. Gale and Stos-Gale 1981, 104–15; Crowfoot Payne 1993, 14, 139, no. 1155, 141–42, no. 1180; Gale and Stos-Gale 1993, 255.
11. Philip and Rehren 1996, 140.
12. Gale and Stos-Gale 1981, 103–104; Boyle 1987, 24.
13. Boyle 1987, 584–87.
14. Gale and Stos-Gale 1981, 110.
15. Lucas and Harris 1962, 491.
16. Hassan and Hassan 1981, 77–82; Crowfoot Payne 1993, 141, no. 1180.
17. See respectively, Prag 1978, 37–38; Vaux 1951, 587, fig. 13; and Ben-Tor 1975, 26, 29.
18. Philip and Rehren 1996, 129–31.
19. Voigt and Dyson 1992, 1:127, and 2: fig. 2.
20. Schmidt 1937, 121, 129.
21. Lenzen 1958, 33; Moorey 1985, 114.
22. Prag 1978, 39–40.
23. Ibid., 39; Stech and Pigott 1986, 51.
24. Prag 1986, 72.
25. Moorey 1985, 108.
26. Gale and Stos-Gale 1981, 115. For Tell Sotto, see Merpert and Munchaev 1993, 245. Because of the close proximity of Tell Sotto and Yarim Tepe, Tell Sotto does not appear on the maps.
27. Bar-Adon 1980, 2; Gates 1992, 131.
28. Key 1980, 241.
29. Tadmor 1989, 250–61; Gates 1992, 131–39.
30. Gale and Stos-Gale 1981, 115.
31. Crowfoot Payne 1993, 14, 141–42.
32. Philip and Rehren 1996, 143.

33. Schmidt 1937, 122–23; see also Stech and Pigott 1986, 49.
34. Petrie 1915, 44; Crowfoot Payne 1968, 58–61.
35. Bar-Adon 1980, 150.
36. Crowfoot Payne 1968, 58.
37. Herrmann 1968, 21–22, 28–31; Ratnagar 1981, 135.
38. Lenzen 1958, 31.
39. Herrmann 1968, 21–22, 28–31; Ratnagar 1981, 135.
40. Bar-Adon 1980, 150.
41. Kaczmarczyk and Hedges 1983, A71–A78.
42. Tobler (1950, 88) describes the faience as white paste; Moorey 1985, 143.
43. Driel and Driel-Murray 1979, 19–20.
44. Quibell 1900, 7; Quibell and Green 1902, 38; Garstang 1907, 135.
45. Porada 1980, 178–80.
46. Weiss and Young 1975, 14–16.
47. Herrmann 1968, 36.
48. Smith 1991, 108.
49. Crowfoot Payne 1968, 58.
50. Smith 1991, 108.
51. Shinnie 1991, 49.
52. Lucas and Harris 1962, 224–25.
53. Shinnie 1991, 49; Smith 1991, 108.
54. Crowfoot Payne 1968, 58.
55. Dreyer 1992, 297; Way 1992, 6–7; Lucas and Harris 1962, 327–37, 391, 404.
56. Porada 1965, 157–58.
57. Mallowan 1947, 36–38, 53.
58. Klem and Klem 1994, 193–96.
59. Petrie 1915, 27; Baumgartel 1960, 1–4.
60. Bard 1987, 195.
61. Philip and Rehren 1996, 140–41.
62. Prag 1978, 37–38.
63. Lenzen 1958, 31, 33; Moorey 1985, 76.
64. Moorey 1985, 76.
65. Ibid., 76; Stech and Pigott 1986, 46, 49.
66. Tobler 1950, 88, 90.
67. Lucas and Harris 1962, 491.
68. Gale and Stos-Gale 1993, 255, no. 1180.

CHAPTER 6. MONKEYS AND MACEHEADS

1. Mallowan 1947, 41.
2. Ibid., 98.

3. Petrie 1915, 10; Mallowan 1947, 40–42; Ward 1964, 13; Ratnagar 1981, 149–53.
4. Amiet 1966, 116, 200, figs. 73, 74, 150.
5. Herrmann 1968, 37.
6. Petrie 1915, 10; Mallowan 1947, 40–42; Ward 1964, 13; Ratnagar 1981, 149–53.
7. Petrie 1903, 24.
8. Ibid.
9. Mallowan 1947, 102.
10. Ibid., 40–41.
11. Schwartz and Weiss 1992, 233–34.
12. Mallowan 1947, 102.
13. Hayes 1965, 109; Elliot 1978, 38; Gonen 1992, 58.
14. Ward 1964, 134–35.
15. Ibid., 19.
16. Ibid., 134–35.
17. Caldwell 1976, 227–40.

CHAPTER 7. CYLINDER SEALS

1. Kantor 1992, 1:15; 2: fig. 6, nos. 48–55.
2. Kantor 1952, 247–49; Ward 1964, 39; Kantor 1965, 11; Collon 1987, 13–14; Kantor 1992, 1:15.
3. Collon 1987, 13–19.
4. Strommenger 1977, 68, 70–71; Driel 1983.
5. Kantor 1952, 249.
6. Mazar 1990, 104.
7. Ben-Tor 1978, 43–45.
8. Ibid., 76–78, 103–105, 108.
9. Ibid., 95.
10. Collon 1987, 140.
11. Boehmer 1974, 495.
12. Podzorski 1988, 262–63.
13. Boehmer 1974, 499–500, fig. 9.
14. Tobler 1950, 191, pls. 168–70.
15. Driel 1983, 38–43.
16. Dreyer with Hartung and Pumpenmeier 1993, 51, abb. 10.
17. Potts 1990, 160–65.

CHAPTER 8. ARCHITECTURE

1. Frankfort 1924, 124–25.
2. Frankfort 1941, 330–39.
3. Spencer 1979, 15–16.

4. Reisner 1936, 27.
5. Spencer 1979, 13–21.
6. Ibid., 15–21.
7. Way 1992b, 222.
8. Petrie, Wainwright, and Gardner 1913, 24–25; Frankfort 1941, 334–36; Emery 1961, 175–77; Clarke and Engelbach 1990, 213–14.
9. Petrie, Wainwright, and Gardner 1913, 24–25. See also, Newberry 1923, 17; Balcz 1930, 38–92; Clarke and Engelbach 1990, 213–14.
10. See respectively, Frankfort 1941, 343; Vinson 1987, 39–81.
11. Emery 1961, 175–78; Badawy 1990, 30–32.
12. See the palette fragment in Hayes 1990, 28–29, fig. 22.
13. Frankfort 1941, 346; Badawy 1948, figs. 9, 71.
14. Frankfort 1941, 343; Emery 1961, 176; See also, Junker 1944, 165; 1947, 102; 1951, 106; 1953, 51, 61.
15. Frankfort 1941, 345; Emery 1961, 178, 189. Tell Billa is located a few kilometers south of Tepe Gawra.
16. Weeks 1972, 29–31.
17. Frankfort 1941, 331, 334–40.
18. Petrie 1974, 54; Spencer 1979, 5.
19. Dreyer with Hartung and Pumpenmeier 1993, fig. 4.
20. Frankfort 1941, 335.
21. Weeks 1972, 31.
22. Frankfort 1924, 136–38; 1941, 358.
23. Emery 1961, 45, 47, 49.
24. Frankfort 1955, 22.
25. Smith 1938, 24–26; Frankfort 1941, 344; Emery 1961, 54–55; Edwards 1978, 42; Spencer 1979, 10–15.
26. Frankfort 1941, 334.
27. Emery 1961, 31, 177.
28. Kantor 1965, 10–11, 15.
29. Way 1987, 247–51. In regard to the clay bottles, also see Perkins 1963, 110–11.
30. Finet 1977, 79, 86–93; Strommenger 1977, 73; Schwartz and Weiss 1992, 1:232–33.
31. Thompson and Hutchinson 1931, 81; Thompson and Hamilton 1932, 78–80.
32. Perkins 1963, 179.
33. Algaze 1986, 126–29.
34. Finet 1975, 162.
35. Petrie 1974, 24.
36. Kemp 1973, 41.
37. Ibid., 41.
38. Potts 1990, 83.

CHAPTER 9. BOAT MOTIFS

1. Kantor 1965, 10; 1992, 1:15–16.
2. Bénédite 1916, 8–10, 32.
3. Yeivin 1964, 25–27.
4. Smith 1967, 76.
5. Williams and Logan 1987, 248.
6. Vandier 1952, 538.
7. Williams and Logan 1987, 248.
8. Bénédite 1916, 10; Frankfort 1924, 139.
9. See respectively Bénédite 1916, 10; Vinson 1987, 181.
10. Petrie 1915, 19; Vinson 1987, 103–13.
11. Petrie 1915, 19.
12. Boehmer 1974b, 36–37.
13. Bénédite 1916, 5.
14. Kantor 1990, 17.
15. Way 1987, 247–51.
16. Quibell and Green 1902, 20–22; Case and Crowfoot Payne 1962, 5–18; Crowfoot Payne 1973, 31–35.
17. See respectively Childe 1953, 80; Petrie 1917, 35; Frankfort 1924, 140; Frankfort 1951, 79; Kantor 1944, 116.
18. Kantor 1944, 122.
19. Winkler 1938, pls. 33.8, 35.16, 36.23, 36.24, 39.38, 40.43, 46.76, 47.80, 48.92, 48.93.
20. See respectively Smith and Simpson 1981, 31; Williams and Logan 1987, 253–57, 271–72.
21. Winkler 1938, 38.
22. Ibid., 27.
23. Winkler 1939, pls. 37–41.
24. Hoffman 1991, 245.
25. Compare the following works, Dunbar 1934; Engelmayer 1965; Basch and Gorbea 1968; Červíček 1986. For a review of this problem see Vinson 1987, 124–62.
26. Winkler 1938, 14, 34.
27. Ibid., 28–29, 31–34.
28. Ibid., 26–28, 34.
29. Ibid., 24–26, 30–31, 34.
30. Ibid., 18–24, 29–30, 34.

CHAPTER 10. THE NARMER PALETTE

1. Ward 1963, 11–13; Ward 1969, 205–11.
2. Yadin 1955, 2.
3. Fairservis 1991, 20.
4. Fischer 1962, 7–25.

5. Ibid., 7, 13, n. 45.
6. Bleeker 1973, 30, 75.
7. Petrie 1900, pl. 27.71; Petrie 1901a, 22, pl. 5.1; Bleeker 1973, 29.
8. Vandier 1952, 595–96.
9. Newberry 1908, 17–19; Vandier 1952, 596; Yadin 1955, 3; Edwards 1978, 3.
10. Gardner 1957, 7.
11. For all entries citing the Sign List, see Gardner 1957, 442–543.
12. See respectively Fairservis 1991, 18; Gardner 1957, 7.
13. Davies 1900, 25; Piehl 1900, 184; Capart 1901, 256; Keimer 1929, 99–101; Vandier 1952, 596; Gardner 1957, 7; Quibell and Green 1902, 43; Fairservis 1991, 11.
14. Davies 1900, 25; Piehl 1900, 184; Capart 1901, 256; Keimer 1929, 99–101; Vandier 1952, 596; Gardner 1957, 7; Quibell and Green 1902, 43.
15. Sethe 1907.
16. Fairservis 1991, 5.
17. Ibid., 11, 20.
18. Williams and Logan 1987, 249.
19. Vandier 1952, 597.
20. Kaiser 1964, 90; Ward 1969, 209–10.
21. Keimer 1929, 99–100; Ward 1969, 209–10.
22. Ward 1969, 206, n. 6.
23. Schott 1950, 22, and text abb. 12.10; Kaiser 1964, 90; Ward 1969, 209.
24. Kaplony 1963, n. 249, fig. 73; Ward 1969, 209.
25. Sethe 1964, 124–28; Edwards 1980, 15–16.
26. Ward 1963, 12; 1969, 210–11.
27. Menes is equated with Narmer or possibly his successor, Aha. See Emery 1961, 32–37; Edwards 1980, 11, 14–15.
28. Emery 1961, 21; Edwards 1980, 2. See also Jeffreys and Malek 1988, 23; Jeffreys and Tavares 1994, 143, 154; Baines 1995, 101.
29. Ward 1969, 206.
30. Bard, 1992, 304.
31. Petrie 1901b, 19, pls. 2.4, 10.1.
32. Gardner 1957, 496.
33. Naville 1903, 215.
34. Junker 1943, 178–79.
35. Yadin 1955, 3–10. For a good review of kites see Helms 1981, 40–47, 50.
36. Mazar 1990, 55.
37. Yeivin 1964, 24.
38. Yeivin 1965, 204–206.

39. Ward 1969, 208–209.
40. Helck 1971, 13–14; Ward 1969, 208, n. 4.
41. Ward 1963, 12.
42. Ward 1969, 210–11.
43. Ibid., 208.
44. Amiran and Gophna 1989, 109–14.
45. Brandl 1989, 379–84; Mazar 1990, 108.
46. Ward 1969, 210.
47. Fairservis 1991, 14–16, 18.
48. Ibid., 12, 18.
49. Capart 1901, 258.
50. Piehl 1900, 184.
51. Petrie 1953, 16.
52. Arnett 1982, 39.
53. Fairservis 1991, 16.
54. Ibid., 16.
55. Petrie 1953, 12–13.
56. Newberry 1908, 20–21.
57. Ibid.; Schott 1950, 23; Vandier 1952, 598; Petrie 1953, 17; Baumgartel 1960, 93.
58. See respectively, Vandier 1952, 598; Frankfort 1924, 120, n. 2.
59. Schott 1952, 25.
60. Yadin 1955, 12–13.
61. Ibid., 13–16.
62. Yeivin 1964, 28–34.
63. Ibid., 33.
64. Newberry 1915, 97–99.
65. Gaballa 1976, 15; Spencer 1993, 53.
66. Weill 1961, 184.
67. Schott 1950, 19–21.
68. Millet 1990, 53–59.
69. Millet 1990, 53.
70. Petrie 1901, pls. 2–8.
71. Millet 1990, 58.
72. Millet 1990, 58.
73. Baines 1995, 125–26.
74. Bard 1992, 300.
75. Spencer 1993, 63–67.
76. Bard 1992, 300.
77. Baines 1995, 125.
78. Baines 1995, 117.
79. Baines 1995, 107–108.
80. Baines 1995, 96, 102–103, 108.

81. Way 1992: 3–5.
82. Köhler 1992, 11–22.
83. Way 1988, 249.
84. Baines 1995, 108.
85. Kantor 1965, 15.
86. Kantor 1992: 17.
87. Kantor 1992, 17.
88. Bleeker 1973, 50–51.
89. Ibid., 72–73.
90. Quibell 1900, 10.
91. Hall 1986, 4.
92. Fairservis 1991, 10.
93. Bard 1992, 304.
94. Hall 1986, 4.
95. Ibid.
96. Petrie 1901, 22, pl. 4.20.
97. Emery 1961, 105.
98. Wainwright 1923, 26–32.
99. Redford 1992, 25; see also Amiet 1961, fig. 282.
100. Quibell 1900, 9.
101. Davis 1989, 162.
102. Smith 1992, 241–42.
103. Ibid.
104. Goff 1963, 66.
105. Weill 1961, 285–86.
106. Emery 1991, 42; Hall 1986, 4; Baines 1995, 114.
107. For example, see Dreyer 1992b, 259.
108. Baumgartel 1960, 103–104, 116–17; Baumgartel 1966.
109. Davis 1989, 162.
110. See also Teissier 1987, 28.
111. Williams and Logan 1987, 247–50; see also Teissier 1987, 28.
112. Williams and Logan 1987, 263.
113. Ibid., 252.
114. According to Williams the Qustul incense burner comes from tomb L 24 and the Horus incense burner comes from tomb L 11. For their chronological order see Williams 1986, 179.
115. Williams 1980, 17–20.
116. Williams 1986, 163–65, 172.
117. Williams 1980, 19–20.
118. Williams 1986, fig. 178g.
119. Williams 1980, 19–20
120. Ben-Tor 1975, 29–30.
121. Williams 1986, fig. 181.

122. Petrie 1915, pl. 51.
123. Frankfort 1924, 127; Quibell 1900, 11.
124. Petrie 1903, 28–29, and pl. xii.273; Adams and Friedman 1992, 329–30, 332.
125. Williams 1986, 123–28. The remains of a similar vase was recovered from the First Dynasty tomb of Neith-hotep. Morgan 1897, 181, fig. 653.
126. Williams 1986, 128; see also El-Khouli 1978, 782.
127. Williams 1986, 128.
128. Ibid., 165. Djer is the third Pharaoh of the First Dynasty.
129. Ibid., 123–28.
130. Ibid., 165, n. 35.
131. Petrie 1901b, 16; Williams 1986, 165, n. 35.
132. See respectively Petrie 1901b, 16; Adams 1984, 9.
133. Petrie 1901b, 17, 37, pl. 35.
134. Williams 1986, 138–45.
135. Heinrich 1936, 15–16.
136. Lauer 1976, 100, 133.
137. Adams 1985, 187.
138. Pomerance 1975, 21–30.
139. Griffiths 1980, 133–34. See also, Mercer 1952, 1: *Pyramid Text* § 1804, and Breasted 1906, 1: § 182.
140. Mercer 1952, 4: *Pyramid Text* § 24–25.
141. Mercer 1956, 41–52; Griffiths 1980, 80.
142. Mercer 1952, 1: *Pyramid Text* § 724, 900, 1012–13, 1624, 1820–21.
143. Mercer 1952, 1: *Pyramid Text* § 1792–96.
144. Frankfort 1955, 43.
145. Mercer 1952 1: *Pyramid Text* § 1703, 2190; Edgar 1911, 87–90; Griffiths 1980, 129–30.
146. Frankfort 1955, 43.
147. Mercer 1952, 1: *Pyramid Text* § 1234; Griffiths 1980, 63.
148. Mercer 1956, 45–46.
149. The translation of this sign ($ꜣꜥꜥw$) is uncertain. Faulkner derives the noun "talkers" by tentatively associating it with the verb ($ꜣꜥꜥ$) "jabber." An alternative meaning would be "those who speak gibberish," which may strengthen the view that foreigners are being described, or that Lower Egyptians spoke a different language or dialect. Moret translates this ideogram as "foreigners" and Sethe as "Quellenorten" (place where things come from). See respectively Faulkner 1986, 91, n. 13; Moret 1972, 77; Sethe 1962, 244.
150. Faulkner 1986, 90.
151. Gardner 1947, 118.
152. Frankfort 1955, 84.

153. Dreyer 1992b, 259–60; see also Griffiths 1980, 153, n. 13.
154. Gardner 1947, 118.
155. Ibid., 117.
156. Frankfort 1955, 87.
157. Gardner 1947, 117.
158. Mercer 1956, 44–45.
159. Frankfort 1955, 42, 86.
160. Ibid., 92.
161. Breasted 1906, 2:96, n. 235.
162. Edwards 1980, 16.
163. Mercer 1952, 1: *Pyramid Text* § 1004–1005, 1013, 1089; Mercer 1952, 4:89–90.
164. Griffiths 1980, 21.
165. Frankfort 1955, 76.
166. Frankfort 1939, pl. 3d.
167. Yeivin 1964, 23, n. 4.
168. Junker 1944, 165; 1947, 102; 1951, 106; 1953, 51, 61.
169. Ward 1969, 210–11.
170. Kantor 1992, I:15, 17.
171. Goff 1963, figs. 277, 278.

CHAPTER 11. TRADE ROUTES

1. Bass 1972, 12.
2. Simmons and Reese 1993, 41.
3. Thuesen 1988, 186–87.
4. Oates 1993a, 171.
5. Porada et al. 1992, 1:95.
6. Weiss 1989, 597.
7. Sürenhagen 1986, 21–22.
8. Schwartz 1989, 593.
9. Tobler 1950, 7.
10. Helms 1977, 27–30; 1987, 51–77.
11. Pulak 1992, 5, 7–10.
12. Bass et al. 1989, 11.
13. Bass 1986, 269.
14. Pulak 1988, 26–27.
15. Pulak 1992, 8–9, 11.
16. Pulak 1994, 9.
17. Peachey 1996, 6.
18. Casson 1971, 285–86.
19. Prag 1986, 59.
20. Kantor 1992, 1:16.
21. Ibid.

22.   Lamberg-Karlovsky 1989, 596.
23.   Kantor 1992, I:16.
24.   Potts 1990, 62–92.
25.   Ward 1963, 7–9.
26.   Kantor 1965, 15.
27.   Richard 1987, 30.

BIBLIOGRAPHY

Adams, B. 1984. *Egyptian mummies.* Bucks, England: Shire Publications.

Adams, B., and R. F. Friedman. 1992. Imports and influences in the Predynastic and Protodynastic settlement and funerary assemblages at Hierakonpolis. In *The Nile Delta in transition: 4th–3rd millennium* B.C. Edited by E. C. M. van den Brink. Pp. 317–38. Jerusalem: E. C. M. van den Brink.

Adams, W. Y. 1985. Doubts about the "Lost Pharaohs." *Journal of Near Eastern Studies* 44: 185–92.

Algaze, G. 1986a. Habuba on the Tigris: Archaic Nineveh reconsidered. *Journal of Near Eastern Studies* 45: 125–35.

———. 1986b. Kurban Höyük and the Late Chalcolithic period in the northwest Mesopotamian periphery: A preliminary assessment. In *Ǧamdat Nasr: Period or regional style?* Edited by Tübingen Atlas zur Vorderen Orient. U. Finkerbeiner and W. Röllig. Pp. 274–315. Wiesbaden: Dr. Ludwig Reichert Verlag.

———. 1989. The Uruk expansion. *Current Anthropology* 30: 571–608.

Alden, J. R. 1982. Trade and politics in Proto-Elamite Iran. *Current Anthropology* 23: 613–38.

Al Khalifa, S. H. A., and M. Rice, eds. 1986. *Bahrain through the ages.* London: Kegan Paul.

Amiet, P. 1961. *La glyptique mesopotamienne archaïque.* Paris: Editions du centre national de la recherche scientifique.

———. 1966. *Elam.* Auvers-Surs-Oise: Archée Éditeur.

———. 1972. *Glyptique susienne des origines à l'époque des Perses Achéménides: Cachets, sceaux cylindres et empreintes antiques découverts à Suse de 1913–1967.* 2 Volumes. Délégation archéologique française en Iran, Memoire 43. Paris: Paul Geuthner.

———. 1975. A cylinder seal impression found at Umm an-Nar. *East and West* 25: 425–27.

———. 1980. *Art of the ancient Near East*. New York: Harry N. Abrams.

Amin, M. A. 1970. Ancient trade and trade routes between Egypt and the Sudan, 4000 to 700 B.C. *Sudan Notes and Records* 51: 23–30.

Amiran, R. 1952. Connections between Anatolia and Palestine in the Early Bronze Age. *Israel Exploration Journal* 2: 89–103.

———. 1970a. *Ancient pottery of the Holy Land*. New Brunswick, N.J.: Rutgers University Press.

———. 1970b. The beginnings of urbanization in Canaan. In *Near Eastern archaeology in the twentieth century: Essays in honor of Nelson Glueck*. Edited by J. A. Sanders. Pp. 83–100. New York: Doubleday.

———. 1974. An Egyptian jar fragment with the name of Narmer from Arad. *Israel Exploration Journal* 24: 4–12.

———. 1985. Canaanite merchants in tombs of the Early Bronze Age I at Azor. *Atiqot* 17: 190–92.

———. 1992. Petrie's F-Ware. In *The Nile Delta in transition: 4th–3rd millennium B.C.* Edited by E. C. M. van den Brink. Pp. 427–32. Jerusalem: E. C. M. van den Brink.

Amiran, R., and R. Gophna. 1989. Urban Canaan in the Early Bronze II and III periods—emergence and structure. In *L'urbanization de la Palestine à l'âge du Bronze ancien*. British Archaeological Reports, International Series 527(i). Edited by P. de Miroschedji. Pp. 109–16. Oxford: British Archaeological Reports.

Anati, E. 1962. Prehistoric trade and the puzzle of Jericho. *Bulletin of the American Schools of Oriental Research* 167: 25–31.

Arkell, A. J. 1963. Was King Scorpion Menes? *Antiquity* 37: 31–35.

Arne, T. J. 1945. *Excavations at Shah Tepé, Iran*. Reports from the scientific expedition to the north-western provinces of China under the leadership of Dr. Sven Hedin. The Sino-Swedish Expedition. Publication 27. Göteborg: Elanders Boktryckeri Aktiebolag.

Arnett, W. S. 1982. *The Predynastic origin of Egyptian hieroglyphs*. Washington, D.C.: University Press of America.

Ayrton, E. R., and W. L. S. Loat. 1911. *Pre-Dynastic cemetery at El Mahasna*. Egypt Exploration Fund 31. London: Egypt Exploration Fund.

Badawy, A. 1948. *Le Dessin architectural chez les anciens égyptienns*. Cairo: Service des antiquités de l'Égypte.

———. 1990. *A history of Egyptian architecture*. Vol. 1. London: Histories and Mysteries of Man.

Baines, J. 1995. Origins of Egyptian kingship. In *Ancient Egyptian kingship*. Edited by D. O'Connor and D. P. Silverman. Pp. 95–156. New York: E. J. Brill.

Balcz, H. 1930. Die Altägyptische Wandgliederung. *Mitteilungen des Deutschen Archäologischen Instituts, Abteilung Kairo* 1: 38–92.

Banks, K. M. 1980. Ceramics of the Western Desert: The Fayum. In *Prehistory of the Eastern Sahara*. Edited by F. Wendorf and R. Schild. Pp. 310–11. New York: Academic Press.

Bar-Adon, P. 1980. *The cave of the treasure*. Jerusalem: Israel Exploration Society.

———. 1980. The trace-element composition of the copper and copper alloys, artifacts of the Nahal Mishmar hoard, appendix E. In *The cave of the treasure*. Pp. 238–43. Jerusalem: Israel Exploration Society.

Bard, K. 1987. *An analysis of the Predynastic cemeteries of Nagada and Armant in terms of social differentiation: The origin of the state in Predynastic Egypt*. Ph.D. diss., University of Toronto.

———. 1992. Origins in Egyptian writing. In *The followeres of Horus: studies dedicated to Michael Allen Hoffman 1944–1990*. Edited by R. Friedman and B. Adams. Egyptian Studies Association Publication No. 2, Oxbow Monograph 20. Pp. 297–306. Oxford: Oxbow Books.

Barnett, R. D. 1958. Early shipping in the Near East. *Antiquity* 32: 220–30.

Barta, W. 1973. *Untersuchungen zum Götterkreis der Neunheit*. Münchner Ägyptologische Studien, Heft 28. Berlin: Bruno Hessling.

Basch, L. 1987. *Le musée imaginaire de la marine antique*. Athens: Institut hellénique pour la préservation de la tradition nautique.

Basch, M. A., and M. A. Gorbea. 1968. *Estudios de arte rupestre nubio*. Vol. 1. *Yacimientos situados en la orilla oriental del Nilo, entre Nag Kolorodna y Kars Ibrim (Nubia egipcia)*. Memorias de la Misión Arqueológica Española en Egipto, Memorias 10. Madrid: Memorias de la Misión Arqueológica Española en Egipto.

Bass, G. F. 1972. The earliest seafarers in the Mediterranean and the Near East. In *A history of seafaring*. Edited by G. F. Bass. Pp. 11–36. New York: Walker and Company.

———. 1986. A Bronze Age shipwreck at Ulu Burun (Kaş): 1984 campaign. *American Journal of Archaeology* 90: 269–96.

Bass, G. F., et al. 1989. The Bronze Age shipwreck at Ulu Burun: 1986 campaign. *American Journal of Archaeology* 93: 1–29.

Baumgartel, E. 1955. *The cultures of prehistoric Egypt*. London: Oxford University Press.

———. 1960. *The cultures of prehistoric Egypt*. Vol. 2. London: Oxford University Press.

———. 1966. Scorpion and rosette and the fragment of the large Hierakonpolis mace head. *Zeitschrift für ägyptische Sprache und Altertumskunde* 93: 9–13.

———. 1974. Predynastic Egypt. In *The Cambridge ancient history*. Edited by I. E. S. Edwards, C. J. Gadd, and N. G. L. Hammond. Vol. 1, part 1, pp. 463–97. Cambridge: Cambridge University Press.

Beck, P. 1984. The seals and stamps of early Arad. *Tel Aviv* 11: 97–114.

Beit-Arieh, I. 1984. New evidence on the relations between Canaan and Egypt during the Proto-Dynastic period. *Israel Exploration Journal* 34: 20–23.

Bénédite, G. 1916. Le couteau de Gebel el-Arak. *Monuments et mémoires publiés par l'Académie des inscriptions et belles lettres, Fondation Piot* 22: 1–34.

———. 1918. The Carnarvon ivory. *Journal of Egyptian Archaeology* 5: 1–15, 225–41.

Ben-Tor, A. 1975. Two burial caves of the Proto-Urban period at Azor. *QEDEM*. Monographs of the Institute of Archaeology 1: 1–53.

———. 1976. A cylinder seal from 'En Besor. *Atiqot* 11: 13–15.

———. 1978. *Cylinder seals of the third-millenium Palestine*. Bulletin of the American Schools of Oriental Research, Supplemental Series 22. Cambridge: American Schools of Oriental Research.

———. 1982. The relations between Egypt and the Land of Canaan during the third millennium B.C. *Journal of Jewish Studies* 33: 3–18.

———. 1986. The trade relations of Palestine in the Early Bronze Age. *Journal of the Economic and Social History of the Orient* 29: 1–27.

———. 1989. Byblos and Early Bronze I Palestine. In *L'urbanization de la Palestine à l'âge du Bronze ancien*. British Archaeological Reports, International Series 527(i). Edited by P. de Miroschedji. Pp. 41–52. Oxford: British Archaeological Reports.

———. 1991. New light on the relations between Egypt and Southern Palestine during the Early Bronze Age. *Bulletin of the American Schools of Oriental Research* 281: 3–10.

Ben-Tor, A., ed. 1992. *The archaeology of ancient Israel*. New Haven: Yale University Press.

Bissing, W. von. 1929. Probleme der ägyptischen Vorgeschichte I: Äegypten und Mesopotamien. *Archiv für Orientforschung* 5: 49–81.

———. 1943. Ägyptische und mesopotamische Siegelzylinder des III Jahrtausends vor Christus. *Nachrichten von der Akademie der Wissenschaften in Göttingen* 6: 481–516.

Bleeker, C. J. 1973. *Hathor and Thoth: Two key figures of the ancient Egyptian religion*. Studies in the History of Religions. Leiden: E. J. Brill.

Boehmer, R. M. 1974a. Orientalische Einflüsse auf verzierten Messergriffen aus dem prädynastischen Ägypten. *Archaeologische Mitteilungen aus Iran* 7: 15–40.

———. 1974b. Das Rollsiegel im prädynastischen Ägypten. *Archäologischer Anzeiger* 4: 496–514.

Borchardt, L. 1898. Das Grab des Menes. *Zeitschrift für ägyptische Sprache und Altertumskunde* 36: 87–105.

Boyle, R. W. 1987. *Gold: History and genesis of deposits*. Society of Economic

Geologist and Society of Economic Geologist Foundation. New York: Van Nostrand Reinhold Company.

Braidwood, R. J. 1939. A note on a multiple-brush device used by Near Eastern potters of the fourth millennium B.C. *Man* 39: 192–94.

Braidwood, R. J., and L. S. Braidwood. 1960. *Excavations in the plain of Antioch I: The earlier assemblages, phases A-J.* Oriental Institute Publications 61. Chicago: University of Chicago Press.

Brandl, B. 1989. Observations on the Early Bronze Age strata of Tel Erani. In *L'urbanization de la Palestine à l'âge du Bronze ancien.* British Archaeological Reports, International Series 527(i). Edited by P. de Miroschedji. Pp. 357–88. Oxford: British Archaeological Reports.

———. 1992. Evidence for Egyptian colonization of the southern coastal plain and lowlands of Canaan during the Early Bronze I period. In *The Nile Delta in transition: 4th–3rd millennium* B.C. Edited by E. C. M. van den Brink. Pp. 441–76. Jerusalem: E. C. M. van den Brink.

Breasted, J. H. 1906. *Ancient records of Egypt: Historical documents from the earliest times to the Persian conquest.* Vols. 1–4. Chicago: University of Chicago Press.

Breton, L. Le. 1957. The early periods at Susa, Mesopotamian relations. *Iraq* 19: 79–124.

Brewer, D. J. 1989. *Fishermen, hunters and herders: Zooarchaeology in the Fayum, Egypt (ca. 8200–5000 BP).* British Archaeological Reports, International Series 478. Oxford: British Archaeological Reports.

Brewer, D. J., and R. F. Friedman. 1989. *Fish and fishing in ancient Egypt.* Warminster, England: Aris and Phillips.

Brunton, G. 1937. *Mostagedda and the Tasian culture.* British Museum Expedition to Middle Egypt, 1928, 1929. London: B. Quaritch.

———. 1948. *Matmar.* British Museum Expedition to Middle Egypt, 1929–31. London: B. Quaritch.

Brunton, G., and G. Caton-Thompson. 1928. *The Badarian civilization and Predynastic remains near Badari.* British School of Archaeology in Egypt and Egyptian Research Account 46. London: B. Quaritch.

Budge, E. A. W. 1972. *From fetish to god in ancient Egypt.* New York: Benjamin Blom.

Burkholder, G. 1972. Ubaid sites and pottery in Saudi Arabia. *Archaeology* 25: 264–69.

Butzer, K. W. 1976. *Early hydraulic civilization in Egypt: A study in cultural ecology.* Chicago: University of Chicago Press.

Caldwell, D. H. 1976. The early glyptic of Gawra, Giyan and Susa, and the development of long distance trade. *Orientalia* 45: 227–50.

Capart, J. 1901. La fête de frapper les Anou. *Revue de l'histoire des religions* 43: 249–74.

————. 1905. *Primitive art in Egypt*. London: H. Grevel.

Case, H., and J. Crowfoot Payne. 1962. Tomb 100: The decorated tomb at Hierakonpolis. *Journal of Egyptian Archaeology* 48: 5–18.

Casini, M. 1984. Neolithic and Predynastic in the Fayum. In *Origin and early development of food-producing cultures in North-Eastern Africa*. Edited by L. Krzyżaniak and M. Kobusiewicz. Pp. 199–204. Poznań, Poland: Polish Academy of Sciences.

Casson, L. 1971. *Ships and seamanship in the ancient world*. Princeton: Princeton University Press.

Caton-Thompson, G., and E. W. Gardner. 1934. *The Desert Fayum*. London: Royal Anthropological Institute of Great Britain and Ireland.

Červíček, P. 1986. *Rock pictures of Upper Egypt and Nubia*. Supplement 46.1 to *ANNALI*, Istituto Universitario Orientale. Rome: Herder.

Childe, V. G. 1953. *New light on the most ancient East*. New York: Frederick A. Praeger.

Clarke, S., and R. Engelbach. 1990. *Ancient Egyptian construction and architecture*. New York: Dover.

Collon, D. 1987. *First impressions: Cylinder seals in the ancient Near East*. Chicago: University of Chicago Press.

Crawford, H. E. W. 1973. Mesopotamia's invisible exports in the third millennium B.C. *World Archaeology* 5: 232–39.

Crowfoot Payne, J. 1968. Lapis lazuli in early Egypt. *Iraq* 30: 58–61.

————. 1973. Tomb 100: The decorated tomb at Hierakonpolis confirmed. *Journal of Egyptian Archaeology* 59: 31–35.

————. 1993. *Catalogue of the Predynastic Egyptian collection in the Ashmolean Museum*. Oxford: Oxford University Press.

Dagnan-Ginter, A., et al. 1984. Excavations in the region of Qasr el-Sagha, 1981 contribution to the Neolithic period, Middle Kingdom settlement and chronological sequences in the Northern Fayum Desert. *Mittleilungen des deutschen archäologischen Instituts, Abteilung Kairo* 40: 33–102.

Davies, N. de G. 1900. *The mastaba of Ptahhetep and Akhethetep at Saqqareh*. Vol. 1. Archaeological Survey of Egypt 8. London: Egypt Exploration Fund.

Davis, W. 1989. *The canonical tradition in ancient Egyptian art*. Cambridge: Cambridge University Press.

Debono, F., and B. Mortensen. 1990. *El Omari: A Neolithic settlement and other sites in the vicinity of Wadi Hof, Helwan*. Mainz am Rhein: Verlag Philipp von Zabern.

Derricourt, R. M. 1971. Radiocarbon chronology for Egypt and North Africa. *Journal of Near Eastern Studies* 30: 271–92.

Dothan, M. 1953. High, loop-handled cups and the early relations between Mesopotamia, Palestine, and Egypt. *Palestine Exploration Quarterly* 85: 132–37.

Dreyer, G. 1992a. Recent discoveries in the U-Cemetery at Abydos. In *The Nile Delta in transition: 4th–3rd millennium B.C.* Edited by E. C. M. van den Brink. Pp. 293–300. Jerusalem: E. C. M. van den Brink.

———. 1992b. Horus Krokodil, ein Gegenkönig der Dynastie O. In *The Followers of Horus: Studies Dedicated to Michael Allen Hoffman 1944–1990.* Edited by R. Friedman and B. Adams. Egyptian Studies Association Publication No. 2, Oxbow Monograph 20. Pp. 259–63. Oxford: Oxbow Books.

Dreyer, G., with U. Hartung and F. Pumpenmeier. 1993. Umm el-Qaab: Nachuntersuchungen im frühzeitlichen Königsfriedhof 5/6. Vorbericht. *Mitteilungen des Deutschen Archäologischen Instituts, Abteilung Kairo* 49: 23–62.

Driel, G. van. 1983. Seals and sealings from Jebel Aruda, 1974–1978. *Akkadica* 33: 34–62.

Driel, G. van, and C. van Driel-Murray. 1979. Jebel Aruda, 1977–1978. *Akkadica* 12: 2–28.

———. 1983. Jebel Aruda, the 1982 season of excavation, interim report (1). *Akkadica* 33: 1–26.

Dunand, M. 1973. *Fouilles de Byblos.* Tome 5. Paris: Librairie ďAmérique et ďOrient Adrien Maisonneuve.

Dunbar, J. C. 1934. Some Nubian rock pictures. *Sudan Notes and Records* 17: 139–67.

During Caspers, E. C. L. 1971. New archaeological evidence for maritime trade in the Persian Gulf during the Late Protoliterate period. *East and West* 21: 21–44.

Edgar, M. C. C. 1911. Notes from the Delta. *Annales du service des antiquités de Ľégypte* 11: 87–90

Edwards, I. E. S. 1978. *The pyramids of Egypt.* New York: Viking Press.

———. 1980. The Early Dynastic period. In *The Cambridge ancient history.* Edited by I. E. S. Edwards, C. J. Gadd, and N. G. L. Hammond. Vol. 1, part 2A, pp. 1–70. Cambridge: Cambridge University Press.

Eiwanger, J. 1984. *Merimde-Benisalâme I: Die Funde der Urschicht.* Deutschen Archäologischen Instituts, Abteilung Kairo. Archäologische Veröffentlichungen 47. Mainz am Rhein: Verlag Philipp von Zabern.

———. 1988. *Merimde-Benisalâme II: Die Funde der mittleren Merimdekultur.* Deutschen Archäologischen Instituts, Abteilung Kairo. Archäologische Veröffentlichungen 51. Mainz am Rhein: Verlag Philipp von Zabern.

El-Khouli, A. 1978. *Egyptian stone vessels: Predynastic period to Dynasty III.* 3 vols. Mainz am Rhein: Verlag Philipp von Zabern.

Elliot, C. 1977. The religious beliefs of the Ghassulians *c.* 4000–3100 B.C. *Palestine Exploration Quarterly* 109: 3–25.

———. 1978. The Ghassulian culture in Palestine: Origins, influences, and abandonment. *Levant* 10: 37–54.

Emery, W. 1939. *Hor-Aha: Excavations at Saqqara, 1937–1938.* Service des antiqutés de Légypte. Cairo: Government Press.

———. 1961. *Archaic Egypt.* Harmondsworth, England: Penguin.

Engberg, R. M., and G. M. Shipton. 1934. *Notes on the Chalcolithic and Early Bronze Age pottery of Megiddo.* Studies in Ancient Oriental Civilization 10. Chicago: University of Chicago Press.

Engelbach, R. 1923. *Harageh.* British School of Archaeology in Egypt 28. London: British School of Archaeology in Egypt and B. Quaritch.

Engelmayer, R. 1965. *Die Felsgravierungen im Distrikt Sayala-Nubien.* Vol. 1: *Die schiffsdarstellungen.* Österreichische Akademie der Wissenschaften Philosophisch-Historische Klasse Denkschriften 90. Vienna: Hermann Böhlaus Nachf./Graz-Wien-Köln.

Fairservis, W. A., Jr. 1991. A revised view of the Na?rmr Palette. *Journal of the American Research Center in Egypt* 28: 1–20.

Faulkner, R. O. 1986. *The ancient Egyptian Pyramid Texts.* Oxford: Clarendon Press.

Finet, A. 1975. Les temples sumeriens du Tell Kannâs. *Syria* 52: 157–74.

———. 1977. Bilan provisoire des fouilles belges du Tell Kannâs. *Annual of the American Schools of Oriental Research* 44: 79–95.

Fischer, H. G. 1962. The cult and nome of the Goddess Bat. *Journal of the American Research Center in Egypt* 1: 7–25.

Forbes, R. J. 1965a. *Studies in ancient technology.* Vol. 2. Leiden: E. J. Brill.

———. 1965b. *Studies in ancient technology.* Vol. 8. Leiden: E. J. Brill.

Frankfort, H. 1924. *Studies in early pottery of the Near East.* Vol. 1: *Mesopotamia, Syria, and Egypt and their earliest interrelations.* London: Royal Anthropological Institute of Great Britain and Ireland.

———. 1939. *Cylinder seals.* London: MacMillian.

———. 1941. The origin of monumental architecture in Egypt. *American Journal of Semitic Languages and Literatures* 63: 329–58.

———. 1951. *The birth of civilization in the Near East.* Bloomington: Indiana University Press.

———. 1955. *Kingship and the gods: A study of ancient Near Eastern religion as the integration of society and nature.* Chicago: University of Chicago Press.

Frankfort, H., and L. Davies. 1980. The last Predynastic period in Babylonia. In *The Cambridge ancient history.* Edited by I. E. S. Edwards, C. J. Gadd, and N. G. L. Hammond. Vol. 1, part 2A, pp. 71–92. Cambridge: Cambridge University Press.

Frifelt, K. 1975a. A possible link between the Jemdet Nasr and the Umm An-Nar graves of Oman. *Journal of Oman Studies* 1: 57–80.

———. 1975b. On prehistoric settlement and chronology of the Oman Peninsula. *East and West* 25: 359–424.

———. 1976. Evidence of a third millenium B.C. town in Oman. *Journal of Oman Studies* 2: 57–70.

Gaballa, G. A. 1976. *Narrative in Egyptian art.* Mainz am Rhein: Verlag Philipp von Zabern.

Gale, N. H., and Z. A. Stos-Gale. 1981. Ancient Egyptian silver. *Journal of Egyptian Archaeology* 67: 103–15.

Gardiner, A. H. 1947. *Ancient Egyptian onomastica.* Oxford: Oxford University Press.

———. 1957. *Egyptian grammar.* London: Oxford University Press.

———. 1961. *Egypt of the pharaohs.* Oxford: Clarendon Press.

Garstang, J. 1907. Excavations at Hierakonpolis, at Esna and in Nubia. *Annales du service des antiquits de lÈgypte* 8: 132–48.

Gates, M. 1992. Nomadic pastoralists and the Chalcolithic hoard from Nahal Mishmar. *Levant* 24: 131–39.

Genouillac, H. de. 1934. *Fouilles de Telloh.* Vol. 1: *époques présargoniques.* Paris: Paul Geuthner.

Ghirshman, R. 1935. *Fouilles du Tépé-Giyan.* Paris: Paul Geuthner.

Goff, B. L. 1963. *Symbols of prehistoric Mesopotamia.* New Haven: Yale University Press.

Goldman, H. 1956. *Excavations at Gözlü Kule, Tarsus.* Vol. 2. Princeton: Princeton University Press.

Gonen, R. 1992. The Chalcolithic period. In *The archaeology of ancient Israel.* Edited by A. Ben-Tor. Pp. 40–80. New Haven: Yale University Press.

Gophna, R. 1976a. Egyptian immigration into southern Canaan during the First Dynasty. *Tel Aviv* 3: 31–37.

———. 1976b. Excavations at 'En Besor. *Atiqot* 11: 1–9.

Gophna, R., and D. Gazit. 1985. The First Dynasty Egyptian residency at 'En Besor. *Tel Aviv* 12: 9–15.

Griffiths, J. G. 1980. *The origins of Osiris and his cult.* Leiden: E. J. Brill.

Habashi, F., and F. A. Bassyouni. 1982. *Mineral resources of the Arab countries.* 2nd ed. London: Chemecon Publishing Limited.

Hall, E. S. 1986. *The Pharaoh smites his enemies: A comparative study.* Münchner Ägyptologische Studien, Heft 44. Berlin: Deutscher Kunstverlag München.

Hall, H. R. 1922. The discoveries at Tell el-Obeid in southern Babylonia and some Egyptian comparisons. *Journal of Egyptian Archaeology* 8: 241–57.

Hanbury-Tenison, J. W. 1986. *The Late Chalcolithic to Early Bronze I transition in Palestine and Transjordan.* British Archaeological Reports, International Series 311. Oxford: British Archaeological Reports.

Harlan, J. R. 1992. Indigenous African agriculture. In *The origins of agriculture.* Edited by C. W. Cowan and P. J. Watson. Pp. 59–70. Washington, D.C.: Smithsonian Institute.

Harrison, J. V. 1968. Minerals. In *The Cambridge history of Iran.* Edited by W. B. Fisher. Pp. 489–516. Cambridge: Cambridge University Press.

Hassan, A. A., and F. A. Hassan. 1981. Source of galena in Predynastic Egypt at Nagada. *Archaeometry* 23: 77–82.

Hassan, F. 1984. Environment and subsistence in Predynastic Egypt. In *From hunters to farmers: The causes and consequences of food production in Africa.* Edited by J. D. Clark and S. A. Brandt. Pp. 57–64. Berkeley and Los Angeles: University of California Press.

———. 1988. The Predynastic of Egypt. *Journal of World Prehistory* 2.2: 135–85.

Hastings, A., J. H. Humphries, and R. H. Meadows. 1975. Oman in the third millenium BCE. *Journal of Oman Studies* 1: 9–55.

Hawass, Z., F. A. Hassan, and A. Gautier. 1988. Chronology, sediments, and subsistence at Merimda Beni Salama. *Journal of Egyptian Archaeology* 74: 31–38.

Hayes, W. C. 1965. *Most ancient Egypt.* Chicago: University of Chicago Press.

———. 1990. *The scepter of Egypt: A background for the study of the Egyptian antiquities in the Metropolitan Museum of Art.* Part 1: *From the earliest times to the end of the Middle Kingdom.* New York: Metropolitan Museum of Art.

Heinrich, E. 1936. *Kleinfunde aus den archäischen Tempelschichten in Uruk.* Leipzig: Otto Harrassowits.

Helck, W. 1971. *Die Beziehungen Ägyptens zu Vorderasien im 3. und 2. Jahrtausend v. Chr.* Ägyptologische Abhandlungen 5. Wiesbaden: Otto Harrassowitz.

Helms, S. W. 1975. Jawa 1973: A preliminary report. *Levant* 7: 20–38.

———. 1976. Jawa Excavations 1974: A preliminary report. *Levant* 8: 1–35.

———. 1977. Jawa Excavations 1975: Third preliminary report. *Levant* 9: 21–35.

———. 1981. *Jawa: Lost city of the Black Desert.* Ithaca, N.Y.: Cornell University Press.

———. 1987. Jawa, Tell Um Hammad and the EB I/Late Chalcolithic landscape. *Levant* 19: 49–81.

Hennessy, J. B. 1967. *The foreign relations of Palestine during the Early Bronze Age.* London: B. Quaritch.

Herrmann, G. 1968. Lapis lazuli: The early phases of its trade. *Iraq* 30: 21–57.

Hoffman, M. A. 1984. Predynastic cultural ecology and patterns of settlement in Upper Egypt as viewed from Hierakonpolis. In *Origin and early development of food-producing cultures in North-Eastern Africa.* Edited by L. Krzyżaniak and M. Kobusiewicz. Pp. 235–46. Poznan: Polish Academy of Sciences and Poznan Archaeological Museum.

———. 1988. *The first Egyptians.* Columbia: McKissick Museum, University of South Carolina.

————. 1991. *Egypt before the pharaohs.* 2nd ed. Austin: University of Texas Press.

Hornell, J. 1941. Sea-Trade in early times. *Antiquity* 15: 233–56.

Ilan, O., and M. Sebbane. 1989. Copper metallurgy, trade, and the urbanization of southern Canaan in the Chalcolithic and Early Bronze Age. In *L'urbanisation de la Palestine à l'âge du Bronze ancien.* Edited by P. de Miroschedji. British Archaeological Reports, International Series 527(i). Pp. 139–62. Oxford: British Archaeological Reports.

Jeffreys, D., and Ana Tavares. 1994. The historic landscape of early dynastic Memphis. *Mitteilungen des Deutschen Archäologischen Instituts, Abteilung Kairo* 50: 143–73.

Jeffreys, D. G., and J. Malek. 1988. Memphis 1986, 1987. *Journal of Egyptian Archaeology* 74: 15–29.

Jesus, P. S. de. 1978. Metal resources in ancient Anatolia. *Anatolian Studies* 28: 97–102.

————. 1980. *The development of prehistoric mining and metallurgy in Anatolia.* British Archaeological Reports, International Series 74 (1, 2). Oxford: British Archaeological Reports.

Johnson, G. A. 1987. The changing organization of Uruk administration on the Susiana Plain. In *The archaeology of western Iran.* Edited by F. Hole. Pp. 107–40. Washington, D.C.: Smithsonian Institute.

Junker, H. 1929. Vorläufiger Bericht über die Grabung der Akadamie der Wissenschaften in Wien auf der neolithischen Siedlung von Merimde-Benisalame (Westdelta). *Anzeiger der Akademie der Wissenschaft in Wien* 66: 156–250.

————. 1930. Vorläufiger Bericht über die Grabung der Akadamie der Wissenschaften in Wien auf der neolithischen Siedlung von Merimde-Benisalame (Westdelta). *Anzeiger der Akademie der Wissenschaft in Wien* 67: 21–83.

————. 1932. Vorläufiger Bericht über die Grabung der Akadamie der Wissenschaften in Wien auf der neolithischen Siedlung von Merimde-Benisalame (Westdelta). *Anzeiger der Akademie der Wissenschaft in Wien* 69: 36–97.

————. 1933. Vorläufiger Bericht über die Grabung der Akadamie der Wissenschaften in Wien auf der neolithischen Siedlung von Merimde-Benisalame (Westdelta). *Anzeiger der Akademie der Wissenschaft in Wien* 70: 54–97.

————. 1934. Vorläufiger Bericht über die Grabung der Akadamie der Wissenschaften in Wien auf der neolithischen Siedlung von Merimde-Benisalame (Westdelta). *Anzeiger der Akademie der Wissenschaft in Wien* 71: 118–32.

————. 1940a. Der Tanz der *Mww* und das Butische Begräbnis im Alten

Reich. *Mitteilungen des Deutschen Instituts für ägyptische Altertumskunde in Kairo* 9: 1–39.

———. 1940b. Vorläufiger Bericht über die Grabung der Akadamie der Wissenschaften in Wien auf der neolithischen Siedlung von Merimde-Benisalame (Westdelta). *Anzeiger der Akademie der Wissenschaft in Wien* 77: 3–25.

———. 1943. *Gîza*. Vol. 6: *Grabungen auf dem Friedhof des Alten Reiches bei den Pyramiden von Gîza*. Akademie der Wissenschaften in Wien Philosophisch-historische Klasse, Band 72 Abhandlung 1. Wien und Leipzig: Hölder-Pichler-Tempsky.

———. 1944. *Gîza*. Vol. 7: *Grabungen auf dem Friedhof des Alten Reiches bei den Pyramiden von Gîza, Der Ostabschnitt des Westfriedhofs*, Erster Teil. Akademie der Wissenschaften in Wien Philosophisch-historische Klasse, Band 72 Abhandlung 3. Wien und Leipzig: Hölder-Pichler-Tempsky.

———. 1947. *Gîza*. Vol. 8: *Grabungen auf dem Friedhof des Alten Reiches bei den Pyramiden von Gîza, Der Ostabschnitt des Westfriedhofs*, Zweiter Teil. Akademie der Wissenschaften in Wien Philosophisch-historische Klasse, Band 73 Abhandlung 1. Wien und Leipzig: Hölder-Pichler-Tempsky.

———. 1951. *Gîza*. Vol. 10: *Grabungen auf dem Friedhof des Alten Reiches bei den Pyramiden von Gîza, Der Friedhof südlich der Cheopspyramide, Westteil*. Akademie der Wissenschaften in Wien Philosophisch-historische Klasse, Band 74 Abhandlung 1. Wien und Leipzig: Hölder-Pichler-Tempsky.

———. 1953. *Gîza*. Vol. 11: *Grabungen auf dem Friedhof des Alten Reiches bei den Pyramiden von Gîza, Der Friedhof südlich der Cheopspyramide, Ostteil*. Akademie der Wissenschaften in Wien Philosophisch-historische Klasse, Band 74 Abhandlung 2. Wien und Leipzig: Hölder-Pichler-Tempsky.

Kaczmarczyk, A., and R. E. M. Hedges. 1983. *Ancient Egyptian faience*. Warminster, England: Aris and Phillips Ltd.

Kaiser, W. 1964. Einige Bemerkungen zur ägyptischen Frühzeit. *Zeitschrift für ägyptische Sprache und Altertumskunde* 91: 87–109.

Kantor, H. 1942. The early relations of Egypt with Asia. *Journal of Near Eastern Studies* 1: 174–213.

———. 1944. The final phase of Predynastic culture: Gerzean or Semainean(?). *Journal of Near Eastern Studies* 3: 110–36.

———. 1949. The cultures of prehistoric Egypt: A book review. *American Journal of Archaeology* 52: 76–79.

———. 1952. Further evidence for early Mesopotamian relations with Egypt. *Journal of Near Eastern Studies* 11: 239–50.

———. 1965. The relative chronology of Egypt and its foreign correlations before the Late Bronze Age. In *Chronologies in Old World archaeology.* Edited by R. W. Ehrich. Pp. 1–46. Chicago: University of Chicago Press.

———. 1992. The relative chronology of Egypt and its foreign correlations before the Late Bronze Age. In *Chronologies in Old World archaeology.* Edited by R. W. Ehrich. 3rd ed. Vol. 1, pp. 3–21. Vol. 2, pp. 2–45. Chicago: University of Chicago Press.

Kaplan, J. 1959. The connections of the Palestinian chalcolithic culture with prehistoric Egypt. *Israel Exploration Journal* 9: 134–36.

Kaplony, P. 1963. *Inschriften der ägyptischen Frühzeit.* Vol. 2. Ägyptologische Abhandlungen 8. Wiesbaden: Otto Harrassowitz.

———. 1964. *Inschriften der ägyptischen Frühzeit.* Vol. 3. Ägyptologische Abhandlungen 9. Wiesbaden: Otto Harrassowitz.

Keimer, L. 1929. Bemerkungen und Lesefruchte zu Altagyptischen Naturgeschichte. *Kemi* 2: 84–106.

Kelly, A. L. 1974. The evidence of Mesopotamian influence in Predynastic Egypt. *Newsletter of the Society for the Study of Egyptian Antiquities* 4: 2–22.

Kemp, B. J. 1973. Photographs of the decorated tomb at Hierakonpolis. *Journal of Egyptian Archaeology* 59: 36–43.

Klem, R., and D. D. Klem. 1994. Chronologischer Abriβ der antiken Goldgewinnung in der Ostwüste Ägyptens. *Mitteilungen des Deutschen Archäologischen Instituts, Abteilung Kairo* 50: 189–222.

Krzyżaniak, L. 1977. *Early farming cultures on the Lower Nile: The Predynastic period in Egypt.* Travaux du centre d'archéologie méditerranéenne de l'academie polonaise des sciences 21. Warsaw: Polish Academy of Sciences.

Lamberg-Karlovsky, C. C. 1972. Trade mechanisms in Indus-Mesopotamian interrelations. *Journal of the American Oriental Society* 92: 222–29.

———. 1989. Comments. *Current Anthropology* 30: 595–96.

Langdon, S. 1921. The early chronology of Sumer and Egypt and the similarities in their culture. *Journal of Egyptian Archaeology* 7: 133–53.

Lapp, P. W. 1970. Palestine in the Early Bronze Age. In *Near Eastern archaeology in the twentieth century: Essays in honor of Nelson Glueck.* Edited by J. A. Sanders. Pp. 101–31. Garden City, N.Y.: Doubleday.

Lauer, J. 1976. *Saqqara: The royal cemetery of Memphis.* London: Thames and Hudson.

Leemans, W. F. 1960. *Foreign trade in the Old Babylonian period, as revealed by texts from southern Mesopotamia.* Leiden: E. J. Brill.

Lenzen, H. 1958. Liste der funde aus dem Riemchengebäude. *Vorläufiger Bericht über die von dem Deutshen Archäologischen Institut und der Deutschen Orient-Gesellschaft aus Mitteln der Deutschen Forschungsgemeinschaft in Uruk-Warka unternommenen Ausgrabungen* 14: 30–35.

Levy, T. E. 1986. The Chalcolithic period. *Biblical Archaeologist* 49: 82–108.

Loud, G. 1948. *Megiddo*. Vol. 2: *Seasons of 1935–39*. Oriental Institute Publications 62. Chicago: University of Chicago Press.

Lucas, A. 1928. Silver in ancient times. *Journal of Egyptian Archaeology* 14: 313–19.

Lucas, A., and J. R. Harris. 1962. *Ancient Egyptian materials and industries*. 4th ed., rev. London: E. Arnold.

Macalistar, R. S. 1912. *The excavation of Gezer, 1902–1905 and 1907–1909*. London: J. Murray.

MacDonald, E. 1932. *Beth Pelet*. Vol. 2. London: British School of Archaeology in Egypt.

Mallowan, M. 1947. Excavations at Brak and Chagar Bazar. *Iraq* 9: 1–259.

———. 1980. The development of cities from al Ubaid to the end of Uruk 5. In *The Cambridge ancient history*. Edited by I. E. S. Edwards, C. J. Gadd, and N. G. L. Hammond. Vol. 1, part 1, pp. 327–462. Cambridge: Cambridge University Press.

Martin, H. P. 1988. *Fara: A reconstruction of the ancient Mesopotamian city of Shuruppak*. Birmingham, England: Chris and Martin Associates.

Mazar, A. 1990. *Archaeology of the land of the Bible 10,000–586 B.C.E.* New York: Doubleday.

Mecquenem, R. de. 1928. *Mémoires de la mission archéologique de Perse*. Vol. 20. Paris: Mission de Susiane.

Mellaart, J. 1966. *The Chalcolithic and Early Bronze Ages in the Near East and Anatolia*. Beirut: Khayata.

Mellink, M. J. 1992. Anatolian chronology. In *Chronologies in Old World archaeology*. Edited by R. W. Ehrich. 3rd ed. Vol. 1. pp. 207–20. Vol. 2, pp. 171–84. Chicago: University of Chicago Press.

Menghin, O., and M. Amer. 1932. *The excavations of the Egyptian University in the Neolithic site at Maadi, first preliminary report (season 1930–31)*. Cairo: Misr-Sokar Press.

———. 1936. *The excavations of the Egyptian University in the Neolithic site at Maadi, second preliminary report (season 1932)*. Cairo: Government Press.

Mercer, S. A. B. 1952. *The Pyramid Texts in translation and commentary*. Vols. 1–4. New York: Longmans, Green.

———. 1956. *Literary criticism of the Pyramid Texts*. London: Luzac and Company Ltd.

Merpert, N. Ya., and R. M. Munchaev. 1993. The earliest evidence for metallurgy in ancient Mesopotamia. In *Early stages in the evolution of Mesopotamian civilization*. Edited by N. Yoffee and J. J. Clark. Pp. 241–48. Tucson: University of Arizona Press.

Millet, N. B. 1900. The Narmer macehead and related objects. *Journal of the American Research Center in Egypt* 27: 53–59.

Moorey, P. R. S. 1982a. The archaeological evidence for metallurgy and related technologies in Mesopotamia, *c.* 5500–2100 B.C. *Iraq* 44: 13–38.

———. 1982b. Archaeology and Pre-Achaemenid metalworking in Iran: A fifteen year retrospective. *Iran* 20: 81–101.

———. 1985. *Materials and manufacture in ancient Mesopotamia: The evidence of archaeology and art. metals and metalwork, glazed materials and glass.* British Archaeological Reports, International Series 237. Oxford: British Archaeological Reports.

Moortgat, A. 1969. *The art of ancient Mesopotamia; the classical art of the Near East.* New York: Phaidon.

Moret, A. 1972. *The Nile and Egyptian civilization.* New York: Barnes and Noble.

Morgan, J. de. 1897. *Recherches sur les origines de l'Égypte: ethnographie préhistorique et tombeau royal de Négadah.* Paris: Ernest Leroux.

Murray, M. A. 1970. *Egyptian sculpture.* Westport, Conn.: Greenwood Press.

Naville, É. 1903. Les plus anciens monuments égyptiens. *Recueil de travaux relatifs à la philologie et à l'archéologie égyptiennes et assyriennes* 25: 199–225.

Needler, W. 1984. *Predynastic and Archaic Egypt in the Brooklyn Museum.* Wilbour Egyptian Monographs 9. Brooklyn: Brooklyn Museum.

Newberry, P. E. 1908. The petty-kingdom of the Harpoon and Egypt's earliest Mediterranean port. *Annals of Archaeology and Anthropology, Liverpool* 1: 17–22.

———. 1915. Ta Tehenu-Olive land. *Ancient Egypt and the East.* Pp. 97–100.

———. 1923. *Egypt as a Field for Anthropological Research.* Liverpool: Proceedings of the British Association for the Advancement of Science.

Nibbi, A. 1985. *Ancient Byblos reconsidered.* Oxford: DE Publications.

Oates, J. 1983. Ubaid Mesopotamia reconsidered. In *The hilly flanks: Essays on the prehistory of southwestern Asia.* Edited by T. C. Young, Jr., P. E. L. Smith, and P. Mortensen. Pp. 251–81. Studies in Ancient Oriental Civilization 36. Chicago: University of Chicago Press.

———. 1993a. Excavation at Tell Brak, 1992–93. *Iraq* 55: 155–99.

———. 1993b. Trade and power in the fifth and fourth millennium BC: New evidence from northern Mesopotamia. *World Archaeology* 24: 403–22.

Oates, J., et al. 1977. Seafaring merchants of Ur? *Antiquity* 51: 221–34.

O'Casey, I., A. S. Maney, and M. Johnson. 1973. *The nature and making of papyrus.* Barkston Ash, Yorkshire: Elemete Press.

Oppenheim, A. L. 1954. The seafaring merchants of Ur. *Journal of the American Oriental Society* 74: 6–17.

Oren, E. D. 1973. The overland route between Egypt and Canaan in the Early Bronze Age. *Israel Exploration Journal* 23: 198–205.

———. 1989. Early Bronze Age settlement in northern Sinai: A model for Egypto-Canaanite interconnections. In *L'urbanization de la Palestine à* l'âge du Bronze ancien. Edited by P. de Miroschedji. Pp. 389–405. British Archaeological Reports, International Series 527(ii). Oxford: British Archaeological Reports.

Oren, E., and Y. Yekutieli. 1992. Taur Ikhbeineh—earliest evidence for Egyptian interconnections. In *The Nile Delta in transition: 4th–3rd millennium* B.C. Edited by E. C. M. van den Brink. Pp. 361–84. Jerusalem: E. C. M. van den Brink.

Palmieri, A. 1981. Excavations at Arslantepe (Malatya). *Anatolian Studies* 31: 101–19.

Payne, J. Crowfoot. 1993. Results of X-ray fluorescence analysis of Egyptian gold and silver. In *Catalogue of the Predynastic Egyptian collection in the Ashmolean Museum.* P. 255. Oxford: Oxford University Press.

Peachey, C. 1996. Continuing study of the Uluburun shipwreck artifacts. *INA Quarterly* 23.1: 4–7.

Perkins, A. L. 1963. *The comparative archaeology of Early Mesopotamia.* Studies in Ancient Oriental Civilization 25. Chicago: Oriental Institute of the University of Chicago.

Perlman, I., and J. Yellin. 1980. The provenience of obsidian from Neolithic sites in Israel. *Israel Exploration Journal* 30: 83–88.

Perrot, J. 1961. Une tombe à ossuaires à Azor. *Atiqot* 3: 1–83.

Perry, F. 1972. *Flowers of the world.* New York: Crown Publishers.

Petrie, H. 1927. *Egyptian hieroglyphs of the First and Second Dynasties.* London: B. Quaritch.

Petrie, W. M. F. 1900. *The royal tombs of the First Dynasty.* Vol. 1. Egypt Exploration Fund 18. London: Egypt Exploration Fund.

———. 1901a. *Diospolis Parva: The cemeteries of Abadiyeh and Hu, 1898–99.* Egypt Exploration Fund 20. London: Egypt Exploration Fund.

———. 1901b. *The royal tombs of the First Dynasty.* Vol. 2. Egypt Exploration Fund 21. London: Egypt Exploration Fund.

———. 1902. *Abydos.* Vol. 1. Egypt Exploration Fund 22. London: Egypt Exploration Fund.

———. 1903. *Abydos.* Vol. 2. Egypt Exploration Fund 23. London: Egypt Exploration Fund.

———. 1915. *Prehistoric Egypt.* British School of Archaeology in Egypt 31. London: British School of Archaeology and B. Quaritch.

———. 1917. Egypt and Mesopotamia. *Ancient Egypt and the East.* Pp. 26–36.

———. 1953. *Ceremonial slate palettes.* British School of Archaeology in Egypt 66. London: British School of Archaeology in Egypt and B. Quaritch.

———. 1974. *Naqada and Ballas.* Warminster, England: Aris and Phillips, Ltd.

Petrie, W. M. F., and G. Brunton. 1924. *Sedment.* Vol. 1. British School of Archaeology in Egypt 34. London: British School of Archaeology in Egypt and B. Quaritch.

Petrie, W. M. F., G. A. Wainwright, and A. H. Gardiner. 1913. *Tarkhan*, vol. 1. *Memphis*, vol. 5. British School of Archaeology in Egypt 23. London: British School of Archaeology and B. Quaritch.

Philip, G., and T. Rehren. 1996. Fourth millennium bc silver from Tell Esh-Shuna, Jordan: Archaeometallurgical investigations and some thoughts on ceramic skeuomorphs. *Oxford Journal of Archaeology* 15.2: 129–50.

Piehl, K. 1900. Mélanges. *Sphinx* 3: 183–84.

Piesinger, C. M. 1983. *Legacy of Dilmun: The roots of ancient maritime trade in eastern coastal Arabia in the 4th/3rd millennium* B.C. Ph.D. diss., University of Wisconsin.

Podzorski, P. V. 1988. Predynastic Egyptian seals of known provenience in the R. H. Lowie Museum of Anthropology. *Journal of Near Eastern Studies* 47: 259–68.

Pomerance, L. 1975. The possible role of tomb robbers and viziers of the 18th Dynasty in confusing Minoan chronology. *Studi in onore di Professor Doro Levi. Antichità Cretesi* I. Roma: Università di Catania, Instituto di Archeologica. 21–30, pls. IV–V.

Porada, E. 1965. The relative chronology of Mesopotamia. Part 1: Seals and trade. In *Chronologies in Old World Archaeology.* Edited by R. W. Ehrich. Pp. 133–200. Chicago: University of Chicago Press.

———. 1980. A lapis lazuli figurine from Hierakonpolis in Egypt. *Iranica Antiqua* 15: 175–80, pls. 1–3.

Porada, E., et al. 1992. The chronology of Mesopotamia, ca. 7000–1600 B.C. In *Chronologies in Old World archaeology.* Edited by R. W. Ehrich. 3rd ed. Vol. 1, pp. 77–121. Vol. 2, pp. 90–124. Chicago: University of Chicago Press.

Porat, N. 1992. An Egyptian colony in southern Palestine during the Late Predynastic—Early Dynastic period. In *The Nile Delta in transition: 4th–3rd millenium* B.C. Edited by E. C. M. van den Brink. Pp. 433–40. Jerusalem: E. C. M. van den Brink.

Postel, A. W. 1943. *The mineral resources of Africa.* African Handbooks 2. Philadelphia: University of Pennsylvania Press, University Museum.

Potts, D. T. 1978. Towards an integrated history of culture change in the Arabian Gulf area: Notes on Dilmun, Makkan and the economy of ancient Sumer. *Journal of Oman Studies* 4: 29–51.

———. 1986. Eastern Arabia and the Oman Peninsula during the late fourth and early third millenium B.C. In *Ǧamdat Nasr: Period or regional style?* Edited by U. Finkerbeiner and W. Röllig. Tübingen Atlas zur Vorderen Orient 62. Pp. 137–82. Wiesbaden: Dr. Ludwig Reichert Verlag.

———. 1990. *The Arabian Gulf in antiquity.* Vol. 1. Cambridge: Clarendon Press.

———. 1992. The chronology of the archaeological assemblages from the head of the Arabian Gulf to the Arabian Sea, 8000–1750 B.C. In *Chronol-*

ogies in Old World archaeology. Edited by R. W. Ehrich. 3rd ed. Vol. 1, pp. 63–76. Vol. 2, pp. 77–89. Chicago: University of Chicago Press.

Prag, K. 1978. Silver in the Levant in the fourth millennium B.C. In *Archaeology in the Levant: Essays for Kathleen Kenyon.* Edited by R. Moorey and P. Parr. Pp. 36–45. Warminster, England: Aris and Phillips, Ltd.

———. 1986. Byblos and Egypt in the fourth millennium B.C. *Levant* 18: 59–73.

Pritchard, J. B. 1969. *The ancient Near East in pictures relating to the Old Testament.* Princeton: Princeton University Press.

Pulak, C. 1988. The Bronze Age shipwreck at Ulu Burun, Turkey: 1985 campaign. *American Journal of Archaeology* 92: 1–37.

———. 1992. The shipwreck at Ulu Burun, Turkey: 1992 excavation campaign. *The INA Quarterly* 19.4: 4–11.

———. 1994. 1994 excavation at Uluburun: The final season. *INA Quarterly* 21.4: 8–16.

Qualls, C. 1981. *Boats of Mesopotamia before 2000 B.C.* Ann Arbor, Mich.: University Microfilms International, Dissertation Information Service.

Quibell, J. E. 1898. Slate palette from Hieraconpolis. *Zeitschrift für ägyptische Sprache und Altertumskunde* 36: 81–84.

———. 1900. *Hierakonpolis.* Vol. 1. Egyptian Research Account 4. London: B. Quaritch.

Quibell, J. E., and F. W. Green. 1902. *Hierakonpolis.* Vol. 2. Egyptian Research Account 5. London: B. Quaritch.

Quibell, M. 1905. *Archaic objects.* Catalogue général des antiquités égyptiennes du musée du Caire. Caire: Le Caire imprimerie de l'instisut français d'archéologie orientale.

Ratnagar, S. 1981. *Encounters: The westerly trade of the Harappa civilization.* New York: Oxford University Press.

Redford, D. B. 1992. *Egypt, Canaan, and Israel in ancient times.* Princeton: Princeton University Press.

Reese, D. S., H. K. Mienis, and F. R. Woodward. 1986. On the trade of shells and fish from the Nile River. *Bulletin of the American Schools of Oriental Research* 264: 79–84.

Reisner, G. A. 1936. *The development of the Egyptian tomb down to the accession of Cheops.* Cambridge: Harvard University Press.

Rice, M. 1991. *Egypt's making: The origins of ancient Egypt 5000–2000 B.C.* New York: Routledge, Chapman, and Hall.

Richard, S. 1987. The Early Bronze Age. *Biblical Archaeologist* 50: 22–43.

Rizkana, I., and J. Seeher. 1987. *Maadi.* Vol. 1: *The pottery of the Predynastic settlement.* Deutsches Archäologisches Institut: Abteilung Kairo, Archaeologische Veröffentlichungen 64. Mainz am Rhein: Verlag Philipp von Zabern.

———. 1989. *Maadi.* Vol. 3: *The Non-Lithic small finds and the structural re-*

mains of the Predynastic settlement. Deutsches Archäologisches Institut: Abteilung Kairo, Archaeologische Veröffentlichungen 80. Mainz am Rhein: Verlag Philipp von Zabern.

Roaf, M., and J. Galbreith. 1994. Pottery and P-values: "Seafaring merchants of Ur?" re-examined. *Antiquity* 68: 770–83.

Rosen, S. A. 1988. A preliminary note on the Egyptian component of the chipped stone assemblage from Tel 'Erani. *Israel Exploration Journal* 38: 105–16.

Rostovtzeff, M. 1920. The Sumerian treasure of Astrabad. *Journal of Egyptian Archaeology* 6: 4–27.

Rowley-Conwy, P. 1991. Sorghum from Qasr Ibrim, Egyptian Nubia, *c.* 800 B.C.–A.D. 1811: A preliminary study. In *New light on early farming.* Edited by J. M. Renfrew. Pp. 191–212. Edinburgh: Edinburgh University Press.

Ruskin, A. 1971. *Prehistoric art and ancient art of the Near East.* New York: McGraw-Hill.

Scharff, A. 1926. *Die archäologischen Ergebnisse des vorgeschichtliche Gräberfeld von Abusir el-Meleq.* Wissenschaftlicher Veröffentlichungen der Deutschen Orientgesellschaft 49. Leipzig: J. C. Hinrichs'sche Buchhandlung.

Schmidt, E. F. 1933. Tepe Hissar excavations 1931. *Museum Journal* 23: 323–483.

———. 1937. *Excavations at Tepe Hissar Damghan.* Philadelphia: University of Pennsylvania Press for the University Museum.

Schmidt, K. 1992. Tell el-Fara'in/Buto and el-Tell el-Iswid (South): The Lithic industries from the Chalcolithic to the Early Old Kingdom. In *The Nile Delta in transition: 4th–3rd millennium* B.C. Edited by E. C. M. van den Brink. Pp. 31–42. Jerusalem: E. C. M. van den Brink.

Schott, S. 1950. *Hieroglyphen: Untersuchungen zum Ursprung der Schrift. Akademie der Wissenschaften und der Literatur: Abdhandlungen der Geistes-und Socialwissenschaftlichen Klasse* 24. Mainz am Rhein: Verlag Philipp von Zabern.

———. 1952. Kulturprobleme der Frühzeit Ägytens. *Mitteilungen der deutschen Orient-Gesellschaft* 84: 1–37.

Schulman, A. R. 1976. The Egyptian seal impressions from 'En Besor. *Atiqot* 11: 16–26.

———. 1980. More Egyptian seal impressions from 'En Besor. *Atiqot* 14: 17–33.

Schwartz, G. M. 1989. Comments. *Current Anthropology* 30: 593.

Schwartz, G. M., and H. Weiss. 1992. Syria, ca. 10,000–2000 B.C. In *Chronologies in Old World archaeology.* Edited by R. W. Ehrich. 3rd ed. Vol. 1, pp. 221–43. Vol. 2, pp. 185–202. Chicago: University of Chicago Press.

Sethe, K. 1907. Die Namen von Ober-und Unterägypten und die Bezeichnungen für Nord und Süd. *Zeitschrift für ägyptische Sprache und Altertumskunde* 44: 1–29.

———. 1962. *Übersetzung und Kommentar zu den altägyptischen Pyramidentexten.* Vol. 2. Hamburg: Verlag J. J. Augustin.

———. 1964. Menes und die Gründung von Memphis. In *Untersuchungen zur Geschichte und Altertumskunde Aegyptens.* A reprint of *Beiträge zur ältesten Geschichte Ägyptens.* Pp. 121–41. Hidesheim: Georg Olms Verlagsbuchhandlung.

Shinnie, P. L. 1991. Trade routes of the ancient Sudan 3000 B.C.–A.D. 350. In *Egypt and Africa: Nubia from prehistory to Islam.* Edited by W. V. Davies. Pp. 49–53. London: British Museum Press, in association with the Egypt Exploration Society.

Simmons, A. H., and D. S. Reese. 1993. Hippo hunters of Akrotiri. *Archaeology* 46: 40–43.

Smith, E. B. 1938. *Egyptian architecture as cultural expression.* New York: D. Appleton-Century.

Smith, H. S. 1991. The development of the "A-group" culture in northern Lower Nubia. In *Egypt and Africa: Nubia from prehistory to Islam.* Edited by W. V. Davies. Pp. 92–111. London: British Museum Press, in association with the Egypt Exploration Society.

———. 1992. The making of Egypt: A review of the influence of Susa and Sumer on Upper Egypt and Lower Nubia in the 4th millennium B.C. In *The Followers of Horus: Studies Dedicated to Michael Allen Hoffman 1944–1990.* Edited by R. Friedman and B. Adams. Egyptian Studies Association Publication No. 2, Oxbow Monograph 20. Pp. 235–46. Oxford: Oxbow Books.

Smith, W. S. 1967. Two Archaic Egyptian sculptures. *Bulletin of the Museum of Fine Arts, Boston* 65: 70–79.

Smith, W. S., and W. K. Simpson. 1981. *The art and architecture of ancient Egypt.* New York: Penguin Books.

Speiser, E. A. 1935. *Excavations at Tepe Gawra.* Vol. 1: *Levels 1–8.* Philadelphia: University of Pennsylvania Press.

Spencer, A. J. 1979. *Brick architecture in ancient Egypt.* Warminster, England: Aris and Phillips, Ltd.

———. 1993. *Early Egypt: The rise of civilisation in the Nile Valley.* London: British Museum Press.

Stager, L. E. 1992. The periodization of Palestine from Neolithic through Early Bronze times. In *Chronologies in Old World archaeology.* Edited by R. W. Ehrich. 3rd ed. Vol. 1, pp. 22–41. Vol. 2, pp. 17–60. Chicago: University of Chicago Press.

Starr, R. 1937. *Nuzi.* Vol. 2: *Report on the excavations at Yorgan Tepa near Kirkuk, Iraq, conducted by Harvard University in conjunction with the American Schools of Oriental Research and the University Museum of Philadelphia, 1927–1931.* Plates and Plans. Cambridge: Harvard University Press.

———. 1939. *Nuzi.* Vol. 1: *Report on the excavations at Yorgan Tepa near Kir-*

kuk, Iraq, conducted by Harvard University in conjunction with the American Schools of Oriental Research and the University Museum of Philadelphia, 1927–1931. Text. Cambridge: Harvard University Press.

Stech, T., and V. C. Pigott. 1986. The metals trade in southwest Asia in the third millennium B.C. *Iraq* 48: 39–58.

Stern, E., ed. 1993. *The new encyclopedia of archaeological excavations in the Holy Land.* Vol. 4. New York: Simon and Schuster.

Strommenger, E. 1977. Ausgrabungen der Deutschen Orient-Gesellschaft in Habuba Kabira. *Annual of the American Schools of Oriental Research* 44: 63–78.

Sürenhagen, D. 1977. Untersuchungen zur Keramikproduktion innerhalb der Spät-Urukzeitlichen Siedlung Habuba Kabira-Süd in Nordsyrien. *Acta Praehistorica et Archaeologica* 5–6: 43–164.

———. 1986. The dry-farming belt: The Uruk period and subsequent developments. In *The origins of cities in dry-farming Syria and Mesopotamia in the third millenium B.C.* Edited by H. Weiss. Pp. 7–43. Guilford, Conn.: Four Quarters Publishing.

Tadmor, M. 1964. Contacts between the Amuq and Syria-Palestine. *Israel Exploration Journal* 14: 253–69.

———. 1989. The Judean Desert treasure from Nahal Mishmar: A chalcolithic traders' hoard? In *Essays in ancient civilization presented to Helene J. Kantor.* Edited by A. Leonard Jr. and B. B. Williams. Studies in Ancient Oriental Civilization 47. Pp. 250–61. Chicago: Oriental Institute of the University of Chicago.

Teissier, B. 1987. Glyptic evidence for a connection between Iran, Syro-Palestine, and Egypt in the fourth and third millennia. *Iran* 25: 27–53.

Thompson, R. C., and R. W. Hamilton. 1932. The British Museum excavations on the Temple of Ishtar at Nineveh, 1930–31. *Annals of Archaeology and Anthropology, Liverpool* 19: 55–116, pls. 46–92.

Thompson, R. C., and R. W. Hutchinson. 1931. The site of the palace of Ashurnasirpal at Nineveh, excavated in 1929–30 on behalf of the British Museum. *Annals of Archaeology and Anthropology, Liverpool* 18: 79–112, pls. 17–40.

Thuesen, I. 1988. *Hama: Fouilles et Recherches 1931–1938.* Vol. 1: *The Pre- and Protohistoric periods.* Copenhagen: Nationalmuseets.

Tobler, A. J. 1950. *Excavations at Tepe Gawra.* Vol. 2: *Levels 9–20.* Philadelphia: University of Pennsylvania Press.

Tosi, M. 1976. The dating of the Umm An-Nar culture and a proposed sequence for Oman in the third millenium B.C. *Journal of Oman Studies* 2: 81–92.

Trigger, B. G., et al. 1983. *Ancient Egypt: A social history.* Cambridge: Cambridge University Press.

Ussishkin, D. 1971. The "Ghassulian" temple in Ein Gedi and the origin of the hoard from Nahal Mishmar. *Biblical Archaeologist* 34: 23–39.

———. 1980. The Ghassulian shrine at En-gedi. *Tel Aviv* 7: 1–44.

Vandier, J. 1952. *Manuel d'archéologie égyptienne: les époques de formation.* Paris.

Vaux, R. de. 1951. La troisième campagne de fouilles à Tell el-Far'ah, près Naplouse. *Revue biblique* 58: 393–430, 566–90.

———. 1980. Palestine in the Early Bronze Age. In *The Cambridge ancient history.* Edited by I. E. S. Edwards, C. J. Gadd, and N. G. L. Hammond. Vol. 1, part 2A, pp. 208–37. Cambridge: Cambridge University Press.

Vinson, S. 1987. *Boats of Egypt before the Old Kingdom.* M. A. thesis, Texas A&M University.

Voigt, M. M., and R. H. Dyson. 1992. The chronology of Iran, ca. 8000–2000 B.C. In *Chronologies in Old World archaeology.* Edited by R. W. Ehrich. 3rd ed. Vol. 1, pp. 122–78. Vol. 2, pp. 125–53. Chicago: University of Chicago Press.

Wainwright, G. A. 1923. The red crown in early prehistoric times. *Journal of Egyptian Archaeology* 9: 26–33.

Ward, W. 1963. Egypt and the East Mediterranean from Predynastic and Archaic times. *Journal of the Economic and Social History of the Orient* 6: 1–57.

———. 1964. Relations between Egypt and Mesopotamia from prehistoric times to the end of the Middle Kingdom. *Journal of the Economic and Social History of the Orient* 7: 1–45, 121–35.

———. 1969. The supposed Asiatic campaign of Narmer. *Mélanges de l'Universite Saint-Joseph* 45: 205–21.

———. 1991. Early contacts between Egypt, Canaan, and Sinai: Remarks on the paper by Amnon Ben-Tor. *Bulletin of the American Schools of Oriental Research* 281: 11–26.

Watson, P. J. 1965. The Chronology of North Syria and North Mesopotamia from 10,000 B.C. to 2,000 B.C. In *Chronologies in Old World archaeology.* Edited by R. W. Ehrich. Pp. 61–100. Chicago: University of Chicago Press.

Way, T. von der. 1987. Tell el-Fara'in-Buto: 2. Bericht. *Mitteilungen des deutschen archäologischen Instituts, Abteilung Kairo* 43: 241–57.

———. 1988. Investigations concerning the early periods in the Northern Delta of Egypt. In *The Archaeology of the Nile Delta: Problems and Priorities.* Edited by E. C. M. van den Brink. Pp. 245–49. Amsterdam: Netherlands Foundation for Archaeological Research in Egypt.

———. 1992a. Excavations at Tell el-Fara'in/Buto in 1987–1989. In *The Nile Delta in transition: 4th–3rd millenium* B.C. Edited by E. C. M. van den Brink. Pp. 1–10. Jerusalem: E. C. M. van den Brink.

———. 1992b. Indications of architecture with niches at Buto. In *The Follow-*

ers of Horus: Studies Dedicated to Michael Allen Hoffman 1944–1990. Edited by R. Friedman and B. Adams. Egyptian Studies Association Publication No. 2, Oxbow Monograph 20. Pp. 217–26. Oxford: Oxbow Books.

Weeks, K. R. 1972. Preliminary report on the first two seasons at Hierakonpolis. Part 2: The Early Dynastic palace. *Journal of the American Research Center in Egypt* 9: 29–33.

Weill, R. 1902. Hierakonpolis et les origines de l'Égypte. *Revue archéologique* 41: 117–24.

———. 1961. *Recherches sur la Ire dynastie et les temps prépharoniques*. Vol. 1. Institut français du Caire, Bibliothèque 'Ètude 38. Cairo: Institut français du Caire.

Weinstein, J. M. 1984. The significance of Tell Areini for Egyptian-Palestinian relations at the beginning of the Bronze Age. *Bulletin of the American Schools of Oriental Research* 256: 61–69.

Weiss, H. 1989. Comments. *Current Anthropology* 30: 597–98.

Weiss, H., and T. C. Young. 1975. Godin V and plateau-lowland relations in the late fourth millennium B.C. *Iran* 13: 1–16.

Wenke, R. J. 1984. Early agriculture in the southern Fayum depression: Some test survey results and research implications. In *Origin and early development of food-producing cultures in north-eastern Africa*. Edited by L. Krzyżaniak and M. Kobusiewicz. Pp. 193–98. Poznań, Poland: Polish Academy of Sciences.

Williams, B. 1980. The lost pharaohs of Nubia. *Archaeology* 33: 12–21.

———. 1986. *Excavations between Abu Simbel and the Sudan frontier: The A-group royal cemetery at Qustul, cemetery L*. Oriental Institute Nubian Expedition III, Part 1. Chicago: Oriental Institute.

———. 1987. Forbearers of Menes in Nubia: Myth or reality. *Journal of Near Eastern Studies* 46: 15–26.

Williams, B., and T. J. Logan. 1987. The Metropolitan Museum knife handle and aspects of pharaonic imagery before Narmer. *Journal of Near Eastern Studies* 46: 245–85.

Winkler, H. A. 1938. *Rock-drawings of southern Upper Egypt*. Vol. 1. London: Egypt Exploration Society.

———. 1939. *Rock-drawings of southern Upper Egypt*. Vol. 2. London: Egypt Exploration Society.

Woolley, L. 1955. *Ur excavations: The early periods*. Vol. 4. Publication of the Joint Expedition of the British Museum and of the Museum of the University of Pennsylvania to Mesopotamia. Philadelphia: University Museum.

Wright, G. A. 1969. *Obsidian analyses and prehistoric Near Eastern trade: 7500 to 3500 B.C*. Anthropological Papers no. 37. Museum of Anthropology. Ann Arbor: University of Michigan.

Wright, M. 1985. Contacts between Egypt and Syro-Palestine during the Protodynastic Period. *Biblical Archaeologist* 48: 240–53.

Yadin, Y. 1955. The earliest record of Egypt's military penetration into Asia. *Israel Exploration Journal* 5: 1–16.

———. 1965. *The art of warfare in biblical lands.* Vol. 1. London: Weidenfeld and Nicolson.

Yakar, Y. 1984. Regional and local schools of metalwork in Early Bronze Age Anatolia. *Anatolian Studies* 34: 59–86.

———. 1985. *The later prehistory of Anatolia: The Late Chalcolithic and Early Bronze Age.* British Archaeological Reports, International Series 268 i–ii. Oxford: British Archaeological Reports.

Yeivin, S. 1960. Early contacts between Canaan and Egypt. *Israel Exploration Journal* 10: 193–203.

———. 1963. Further evidence of Narmer at "Gat." *Oriens Antiquus* 2: 205–13.

———. 1964. The ceremonial slate-palette of King Narmer. In *Studies in Egyptology and Linguistics in Honour of H. J. Polotsky.* Edited by H. Rosen. Pp. 22–53. Jerusalem: Israel Exploration Society.

———. 1965. Who were the *Mntyw? Journal of Egyptian Archaeology* 51: 204–206.

Zarins, J. 1989. Ancient Egypt and the Red Sea trade: The case for obsidian in the Predynastic and Archaic periods. In *Essays in ancient civilization presented to Helene J. Kantor.* Edited by A. Leonard Jr. and B. B. Williams. Studies in Ancient Oriental Civilization 47. Pp. 339–68. Chicago: Oriental Institute of the University of Chicago.

INDEX

Note: Pages with illustrations are indicated by italics.

STUDIES IN
NAUTICAL ARCHAEOLOGY

Mott, Lawrence V., *The Development of the Rudder: A Technological Tale*, 1997.

Oertling, Thomas J., *Ships' Bilge Pumps: A History of Their Development, 1500–1900*, 1996.

Simmons III, Joe J., *Those Vulgar Tubes: External Sanitary Accommodations aboard European Ships of the Fifteenth through Seventeenth Centuries*, 1997.